SO MANY SWEET
FLOWERS

SO MANY SWEET
FLOWERS

A SEVENTEENTH-CENTURY FLORILEGIUM

Paintings by Johann Walther 1654

Foreword by Gill Saunders
Edited by Jenny de Gex

PAVILION

FIRST PUBLISHED IN GREAT BRITAIN IN 1997 BY

PAVILION BOOKS LIMITED

26 UPPER GROUND, LONDON SE1 9PD

ANTHOLOGY CONCEIVED, EDITED AND DESIGNED BY

JENNY DE GEX AND DAVID FORDHAM © 1997

FOREWORD © GILL SAUNDERS 1997

INTRODUCTION © JENNY DE GEX 1997

THE TITLE *SO MANY SWEET FLOWERS* IS A QUOTATION FROM

JOHN LYLY'S *EUPHUES AND HIS ENGLAND*

DESIGNED BY DAVID FORDHAM

A CIP CATALOGUE FOR THIS BOOK

IS AVAILABLE FROM THE BRITISH LIBRARY

ISBN 1 85793 353 2

PRINTED AND BOUND BY BOOK PRINT, BARCELONA

TYPESET BY M.A.T.S., SOUTHEND, ESSEX

THIS BOOK MAY BE ORDERED BY POST DIRECT FROM THE PUBLISHER

PLEASE CONTACT THE MARKETING DEPARTMENT, BUT TRY YOUR BOOKSHOP FIRST

CONTENTS

Foreword 7

Introduction 9

THE FLOWERS

Snowdrop 14

Hellebore 16

Narcissus 20

Primula 28

Fritillaria 30

Tulip 36

Ranunculus.............46

Anemone 50

Iris 54

Columbine 60

Peony 62

Geranium 66

Rose 68

Jasmine................74

Lily 76

Poppy 85

Mallow................88

Carnation 90

Oleander................94

Hollyhock 96

Sunflower..............100

Marigold 102

Acknowledgements 104

Snapdragon, pheasant's eye, cornflower, Maltese cross, rose campion

FOREWORD

Horti Itzteinensis

OVER A PERIOD OF TWENTY YEARS Johann Walther painted for his patron the Count of Nassau a sumptuous volume of plant portraits as a record of all the flowers growing in the count's newly created garden at Idstein. This book is known as the *Horti Itzteinensis*, after the garden that it commemorates. One of the two surviving copies is now in the collections of the Victoria & Albert Museum.

Walther's album is one of several printed or painted florilegia produced in the 16th and 17th centuries. The word 'florilegia', which had been used metaphorically to mean an anthology, literally means 'collection of flowers' and in fact these books and albums served as catalogues of collections, for gardens are essentially collections of ephemeral exhibits. Indeed in the 17th century the gardens of aristocrats and virtuosi became living extensions of *Wunderkammern*, and 'cabinets of curiosities', the fashionable collections of all that was strange and wonderful in art and nature.

Trade and travel brought many new plants to Europe in the 16th and 17th centuries, stimulating an interest in creating gardens and acquiring plants. Collectors such as Count Johann of Nassau enthusiastically traded, exchanged, cultivated and hybridized, to bring new and exotic species into their gardens. Unlike the physic gardens (devoted to medicinal plants) which preceded them these flower gardens were haphazard accumulations where the criteria for inclusion were beauty and novelty. Florilegia illustrate only cultivated plants, mostly ornamental varieties. Walther's album is no exception and though his subjects range from the modest - snowdrops and hepaticas - to the dramatic and showy - tulips and paeonies - all are chosen and presented with regard to their decorative character.

Though botanically accurate by the standards of the time, Walther's compositions often impose an artificial symmetry and proximity on their subjects, clumping them together in bouquets or arranging them in sentinel rows. Like a portrait painter he always contrives to show his subjects to their best advantage, elegantly styled and blemish-free. Though they appear to us somewhat stiff and formal, Walther's pictures are an accurate representation of 17th-century planting which favoured mixed beds, with many different species grown together.

Walther's florilegium is virtually unique as a complete record of an actual garden. It was almost certainly inspired by, if not directly modelled on, the magnificent two-volume set of engravings by Basil Besler, the *Hortus Eystettensis*, published in 1613. Besler's book was also the record of an actual garden, that of the Prince-Bishop of Eichstätt. Many of the same species appear in both, and Walther's careful studies find echoes in Besler's supremely decorative plates. The *Horti Itzteinensis* follows other florilegia in arranging the plants in sequence by their season of flowering, beginning with winter-flowering plants such as snowdrops and helllebores and concluding with fruit and vegetables.

The garden recorded so diligently by Walther has long since decayed from neglect but it lives on in these vividly evocative paintings. As they provoke exclamations of pleasure from us, we have a very real sense of the wonder and delight with which flowers were collected and cultivated by Count Johann and his contemporaries.

GILL SAUNDERS, 1997, DEPUTY CURATOR
DEPARTMENT OF PRINTS, DRAWINGS & PAINTINGS
VICTORIA & ALBERT MUSEUM

SIMULACRUM SCENOGRAPHICUM.
Celeberrimi Horti Itzsteinensis
quem fieri fecit
Illustrissimus Comes ac Dominus Dominus IOHANNES Comes Nassouiæ &
Sarapontis. etc.

Populus Alcidæ, Platanus gratissima Xerxi,   Tantorum Heroum Comes æmulus ecce IOHANNES
Regibus Alcinoo & Cyro amor Hortus erat.   Pomonam & Floram Nassoviensis amat.

T. A. S.

THE GARDEN AT IDSTEIN : TITLE PAGE OF THE FLORILEGIUM

INTRODUCTION

THE FLOWER PAINTINGS by Johann Walther are a unique record of the planting of a dream garden created by a 17th-century collector and enthusiast. The date of 1654 marks the first painting of a project and a friendship that was to last until 1674, recorded in correspondence between the artist and his patron, Count Johann of Nassau-Idstein.

The small town of Idstein is situated in south-western Germany, not far from Wiesbaden in the northern Taunus, between the rivers Rhine, Main and Lahn, amidst softly undulating hills and wooded ridges. The castle was linked to the village by a drawbridge. Today it is a school and there is little to see of the former garden fantasy except a space and surrounding walls.

Count Johann came from a branch of the ancient family of Nassau, established in the Lahn region since the 12th century. Through the complexities of titles and inheritance shared between his three surviving brothers, Johann received Idstein in 1629, two years after the death of his father. Nearly twenty years were to pass before he could safely return there, after the Thirty Years War which left the country devastated, burnt and ravaged by civil war and foreign armies. The fighting, famine and pestilence destroyed a third of the population.

In 1648, the treaty of Westphalia placed Germany under Franco-Swedish control. Returning to his lands and castle after twelve years in exile in Strasbourg, to find it completely ruined as a result of wartime atrocities and depredation, Count Johann set about bringing his domain back to life. He restored prosperity to the surrounding region, but also worked on the castle and garden, creating a showcase for his various collections, the passions of his life. In common with other great collectors of the age, he wished to record his collection for posterity. Johann Hoffman from Vienna began this task, which Johann Walther continued: this collaboration lasted for over twenty years, resulting in the *Horti Itzteinensis*, a pictorial record of flowers and fruits grown at Idstein, surviving in two manuscripts, one in the Victoria and Albert Museum and the other in the Bibliothèque Nationale. This makes an almost unique florilegium as a record of an *actual* garden, arranged through the flowering seasons, rather than just a collection of decorative flower paintings.

A possible inspiration was Basilius Besler's *Hortus Eystettensis*, published in 1613, which recorded the garden of Bishop Konrad von Gemmingen, at Eichstätt. Besler was a botanist and apothecary at Nuremberg. Many plants shown in this finest example of plant illustration were later to be found in the collection at Idstein, for Besler's valuable masterpiece was in the count's library.

The Swedish King Gustavus Adolphus sided with the German protestants but after his death in battle the Nassau brothers fled to exile. There is documentary proof of Johann in Metz around 1636, as his seventh and eighth children were born there in 1638 and 1639, when the family moved on to Strasbourg. His first wife died in 1644, having given him eleven children, most of whom were stillborn or died very young. In 1646 he remarried the Countess Anne de Leiningen-Dachsburg, who gave him a further eighteen children, mostly stillborn. When Johann died in May 1677, at the age of 74, from his two marriages he had twenty-nine children, of whom only three survived him, two daughters and a son, born in 1665. The latter was only twelve when his father died, so was placed in the care of a guardian.

Johann of Nassau-Idstein was a typical 17th-century collector, developing his tastes during his years of exile in Strasbourg. Despite reduced circumstances, his art collection contained a total of three hundred works some of which were attribututions to Michaelangelo, Veronese and Cranach. In Strasbourg he met two artists, who also advised him, with whom he developed long-lasting friendships: Sebastien Stoskopff was an acknowledged master of still-life painting and Johann Walther was known as a miniaturist. The term applied not to scale and size, but to the technique of painting, with watercolour heightened by gouache or bodycolour upon vellum, thereby creating an almost three-dimensional effect.

In addition to his paintings, his collection contained quite extraordinary objects in his cabinet of curiosities: minerals, shells, stuffed animals, scientific instruments, telescopes, globes. The fashion for bizarre cabinets was more pronounced in Germany than elsewhere. Fascinated by nature, rich collectors would gather strange treasures for their *Wunderkammern* (literally, rooms of wonders).

To own a library, a picture gallery, a cabinet of curiosities, a garden (in a sense, only an outdoor extension of the others) was all part of a collector's way of life. Johann of Nassau created his fantasy garden following his own designs, prepared during his years of exile, between 1650-1670 when the mania for collecting flowers and fruits reached its zenith. For the 17th century was *the* great period for flower gardens: horticulture had become an aristocratic passion. Records of accounts show that on Johann's return to the castle in 1646 he immediately set to work planting vegetables, and in 1647 considerable sums of money were spent purchasing the first flowers - narcissi, tulips, ranunculus, peonies, and in paying a gardener.

Interest in botany was a new science and fascination, stimulated by the discovery of the New World and resulting plant introductions. Everyone wished to have, and in particular to show off, specimens of rare and sought-after plants, which previously had been considered for their medicinal rather than decorative properties. New plants recently introduced to Europe included hyacinths, narcissi, crown imperials, but the most cherished were lilies and tulips, more for colour and unusual shape than for scent. They had novelty value, and the sense of wonder at these new discoveries is reflected in the language of contemporary 17th-century writers. Many plants came originally from the Mediterranean climates of North Africa and Asia Minor but were fortunately able to settle in the different climates of central European gardens.

Count Johann was in correspondence with friends, acquaintances and relations, with whom he exchanged seeds, bulbs or cuttings, thereby increasing his collection, but gifts alone did not fully stock the garden. Surviving accounts prove that he also purchased plants and bulbs; deliveries of bulbs following the autumn horticultural fair at Frankfurt are recorded, as are purchases from cultivators and plantsmen. Salesmen brought the latest new discoveries from the Dutch ports or from Amsterdam, Antwerp, Brussels or Munich. Thus the

Hyacinthus Stellatus Flore coeruleo:

Arum latifolium:

Arum:

Colchicum Vernum flo pleno purpureum:

FROM HORTUS EYSTETTENSIS, BASILIUS BESLER, 1613

count accumulated his collection of tulips, anemones, ranunculus, irises, narcissi, and carnations.

He corresponded with one of the greatest architects and engineers, Joseph Furttenbach, author of several master works on gardens and architecture, somewhat late in the day, when work on the garden was already well advanced, turning to him for advice on the decoration of the grottoes, and for general approval. There are characteristic signs of Furttenbach's ideas in the design of the Idstein garden: a strictly quadrangular space, surrounded by high walls, a summerhouse and extravagant grottoes, decorated with shells, corals, semi-precious stones, and small carved animals. The

vaulting was painted by Johann Walther, after sketches by Merian, showing the planets orbiting the earth, "as a symbol of the diversity, and as a mirror of, the cosmos."

Yet the most unusual feature of the garden was the shape of the flower beds. Whereas the established rules of garden design decreed they should be in geometric or circular form, often with celestial or astrological symbolism, the count pursued a personal whim and gave them the forms of fruits or vegetables, a fantasy that was quite unique. The count explained in a letter to Furttenbach that his garden was divided into three parts, that in the centre the beds were in the shape of the best fruits such as lemons, peaches, figs, but that towards one

11

side, he gave them the shape of garden enemies, such as caterpillars, and on the other side, extraordinary creatures such as crocodiles or dragons.

Inside these beds, flowers were planted according to contemporary thinking with fritillaries in the centre, lilies at the edge. Next came tulips, planted neatly in rows, interspersed by narcissi and hyacinths. Great care was taken with regard to variety of shape and colour.

Johann Walther was born at the beginning of the 17th century in Strasbourg, then part of Germany but ceded to France by the Treaty of Westphalia at the end of the Thirty Years War. At that time, Strasbourg was the provincial capital of Alsace, a protestant city, and an active artistic centre for an area rich in sculptors, painters and architects. At the age of fourteen, Walther travelled in Germany before going to Holland. In 1625 he went to Paris and Lyon, then on to Switzerland. In 1635 he was established in Strasbourg, where certain German nobles appreciated his talent, in particular Friederich V of Bad-Durlach and Johann of Nassau-Idstein; with the latter he conducted a correspondence that was not restricted only to working relations, ending in 1674. Married in 1628, Walter had fourteen children, of whom two sons continued the profession of their father. In a letter dated 1658 to Johann of Nassau, the painter told his patron of the death of his wife, although he remarried shortly afterwards and survived his second wife. Walther's own death can probably be placed at the end of 1676, when he finished writing his *CHRONIK* of Strasbourg during the Thirty Years War, describing first-hand the attrocities in Alsace, whereby he was known not only as an artist but also as a writer.

Walther visited Idstein at least eight times, either to paint the flowers or for other commissions. The first visit was in 1651, the last in 1672. He travelled by boat down the Rhine until Mainz, usually staying for around six months, from April to September, making sketches from nature during the flowering season which were then completed on his return to Strasbourg. His style of painting is simple and pure, almost naive, and he loved to paint the wonders of nature despite having lived through one of the most terrible periods of European history. Few of his other works survive, an exception being the *Ornithographia* in the Albertina Library in Vienna. It is a collection of a hundred watercolour sketches of birds, painted with scrupulous accuracy between 1639 and 1668.

Count Johann of Nassau-Idstein envisaged a florilegium in two volumes with ninety-six illustrations in each. By 1663, Walther had eleven plates still to complete for the second volume, and with increasing age, found the journey troublesome. The title page showing the allegory of spring was completed in 1666, and on his final visit in 1672 he gave the count his captions relating to the different pictures, texts lovingly designed with initials coloured in black and red in three different types: Latin letters for Latin text, German characters for the German language and brief supplements in Walther's own handwriting. These are a unique feature of the London manuscript and are reproduced here for the first time. The colours and detail in the flowers are exquisite but the manuscript is currently undergoing essential conservation work so will not be available for study or display for some time.

The two surviving manuscripts were perhaps originally one album, the count's own copy, though there are certain duplications between the two. Somehow they were separated and the London copy, bound in two volumes in gold-tooled red calf, came there via the library of the third Lord Bute, a personal friend of King George III , who was "passionately fond of botany". The artist's own copy, which also included details of exactly when each plant flowered and how many blooms it produced, was preserved in the Landesbibliothek at Darmstadt which was destroyed during World War Two.

Florilegia were books developed in the late sixteenth century to illustrate those flowers which were grown for their beauty rather than their medicinal properties. Often the work of professional painters for the royal court or for wealthy patrons, they contain some of the finest representations of flowers ever made. French artists Daniel Rabel and Nicolas Robert were amongst the greatest exponents of flower painting of this kind. The mannered style of a florilegium could leave little scope for originality, but Walther's naive naturalism produced the most appealing studies, richly coloured and with lavish use of bodycolour to give an almost enamelled finish. To create a pleasing composition he often united on a single page several plants that could not have flowered simultaneously in nature. This artistic licence gives further proof that he amalgamated his preliminary sketches to produce the finished plates at a later date. The plants are nevertheless convincingly naturalistic. Although the initial sketches were drawn from nature at Idstein, he completed the paintings at home in Strasbourg. If a particular flower had not been in bloom at the time of his visit, he would use plants from other gardens, or would work instead from published engravings. The florilegia of Crispin van de Passe *(Hortus Floridus)*, Theodore de Bry and Mathew Merian the Elder were all available to him but there is no proof of direct links.

Walther's work is vibrant, straightforward and uncomplicated, his flowers are opulent, blooming and alive. A simple love of life and nature shine through his paintings, mercifully preserved despite the ravages not only of Thirty Years but of a further three hundred years of turbulence .

After the death of Count Johann in May 1677, his son, Georg August succeeded him. Although he did not share his father's passion for flowers, he nonetheless continued to maintain the garden. In 1721 he died suddenly at Biebrich, from smallpox, followed within a few hours by the death of his two daughters. There was no direct descendent and the garden fell into neglect. Today, older inhabitants of Idstein remember finding strange shells, either whole or in fragments, in the earth of the former garden. There is talk of possibly restoring the parterres in the forms of fruits or animals. Meanwhile, the only record of the count's extraordinary fantasy exists in Walther's enduring images.

JENNY DE GEX . 1997

SNOWDROPS

> Sepolitis aliis quibuſcunꝗ, anxiis curis, ſeriis negotiis, moleſtis laboribus, animos & corpora defatigantibus, tranquillæ quieti addictis complaceat, cum elegantiſſima FLORA exſpatiari in viridariumſu, ûm miris modis comptûm, recreandi nos illûs non tam multiplici Plantarûm varietate, qûam verſicolore Florûm amœnitate, qûas ipſa stirpes & rariores, & nobiliores, ex tot provinciarûm, tot diſsitarûm Mundi plagarûm montibus, collibus, ſylvis, hortis, campis, arvis, agris, pratis, ripis, paludibus, rivis, collegit plûrimas; ût per totum Anni circûlum, singûlis Menſibus, alias atque alias virentes & florentes, monſtrare qûeat; adeo, ût nec in Brûma frigore rigente, dûm Boreas alias ſterilis dominatur, non deficiant ex terræ gremio recens nata. Ordine ergo perluſtremûs illas, à Menſe primo uſqûe ad ûltimûm; ex qûibus proxima ſûnt ſeqûentes:
>
> Leucoium bulboſûm, hexaphyllon maius, & Leuconarciſſoliriûm vûlgare. Germanice Groſſe weiſſe Hornungs-Blûmen.

SET APART FROM EVERYTHING, a garden should please those with worrisome cares, difficulties in business, who are exhausted in body and soul and who crave peace and tranquillity. With flowers most elegant in the structure of their foliage, there is wonderful variety in the structure of greenery, invigorating us not only with the great variety of plants but in the multicoloured delight of blooms. It has gathered together from the near and far regions of the world, from mountains, hills, woods, gardens, plains, ploughlands, fields, meadows, riverbanks, marshlands and streams a stock of the rarest and noblest of flowers, so that throughout the whole cycle of the year, it may show, month by month, each one in a state of growth or in flower to such an extent that nothing is ruled by the stiffening cold of the winter solstice when the barren north wind blows, and there is no lack of things new born from the womb of the earth.

Thus we shall progress from the first month to the last: from each follows the next.

HORTI ITZTEINENSIS

THOUGHTS IN A GARDEN

....SUCH WAS THAT HAPPY GARDEN-STATE
While man there walk'd without a mate:
After a place so pure and sweet,
What other help could yet be meet!
But 'twas beyond a mortal's share
To wander solitary there:
Two paradises 'twere in one,
To live in Paradise alone.

How well the skilful gardn'er drew
Of flowers and herbs this dial new!
Where, from above, the milder sun
Does through a fragrant zodiac run:
And, as it works, th'industrious bee
Computes its time as well as we.
How could such sweet and wholesome hours
Be reckon'd, but with herbs and flowers!

ANDREW MARVELL (1621-78)

Pars altera.

SOL.

Vita meúm minús, vitam Sol floribús addo.
Núlla poteſt radiis planta carere meis;
Aúreus à nobis color eſt ſpectandús in hortis;
Et referúnt patrem noſtra creata ſúúm.

LUNA.

Cynthia nocturno flores aſpergo liquore;
Candorem oſtendúnt lilia noſtra ſúúm;
Múltipliciqs comà vacúos effercio flores.
Si fúerit docta coulita planta manú.

MARS.

Grata rúbedo mihi, rúbros Mars profero flores.
Vah quantam ſpeciem flos rúbicúndús habet:
Qúas fúndúnt flammas rútilantia caryophylla:
Flori Romano. quantús habetúr honos

THE SUN
My gift is life and it is life that I, the Sun give to
flowers.
No plant can do without my rays:
The colour of gold seen in gardens comes from me
My creations reflect their source.

THE MOON
I, Cynthia, sprinkle flowers with dew at night.
My lilies display their distinctive radiance.
I fill empty flowers with an abundance of foliage
Providing a cutting has been planted with a skilful
hand.

MARS
Red is my favourite colour: I, Mars, produce red flowers.
Oh what a fine sight a red flower makes:
What flames red carnations pour forth.
The Roman flower is considered to have great honour.

HORTI ITZTEINENSIS

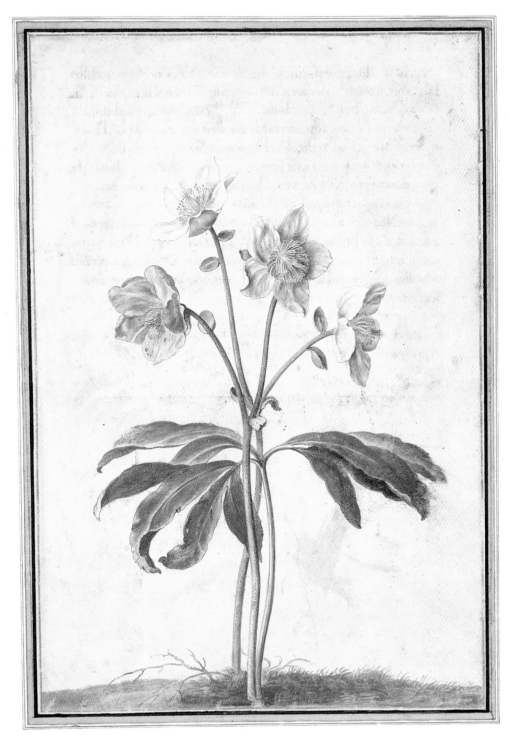

HELLEBORES

CROCUS, GREEN HELLEBORE, CHRISTMAS ROSE, PHEASANT'S EYE, HEPATICA

OF HELLEBORES

The true HELLEBORE with the BLACKE roote and the large WHITE flower, like a single Rose, sometimes dasht with a little red about the edges, with many pale yellow threads standing about a greene head in the middle of the flower. The leaves are thicke and fatt & great & indented, and of a deepe greene color. The stalkes are many, and rise directly out of the earth.

THE GARDEN BOOK OF SIR THOMAS HANMER, 1659

THE CROCUS

THE CROCUS TODAY boasts over seventy known species, but at the time Walther made his paintings, the crocus *vernus* and *sativus* were believed to be the only two, the rest being varieties. Violet and white coloured crocuses that are commonplace today can place their origins in crocus *vernus*, as by the 18th century bulbs were imported in quantity from Holland, and by the 19th century, were grown commercially in Lincolnshire, passed off as "just imported from Holland".

Crocus *sativus*, the Saffron Crocus, has a distinguished history in cultures as different as Mongol, Arab, Roman or Greek, used as medicine, dye or condiment. Wall paintings from the Greek island of Santorini, almost destroyed by volcanic eruption in 1500 BC, show women collecting crocus for the saffron crop. The precious saffron comes only from the dried stigmas: it takes thousands of blossoms to produce a single ounce. The Romans probably introduced the saffron crocus to Britain; later legends tell of a pilgrim bringing a root hidden in his staff to Saffron Walden, where it was cultivated. Bacon noted that 'it maketh the English sprightly' and Tournefort's *Herbal* warned that an overdose may cause people to die of laughing.

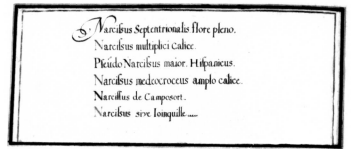

Narcissus Septentrionalis flore pleno.
Narcissus multiplici calice.
Pseudo Narcissus maior. Hispanicus.
Narcissus medeocroceus amplo calice.
Narcissus de Camposort.
Narcissus sive Ioinquille .....

NARCISSUS

THE NARCISSUS IS THE FLOWER longest associated with man: proof of its use by Egyptians in their funeral wreaths has been found in tombs, well-preserved even after the passage of 3000 years. The Greek poets wrote in praise of the narcissus 'wondrously glittering, a noble sight for all, whether immortal gods or mortal men' (Homer) and legends tell how the flower, originally white, was turned yellow by Pluto's touch when he captured the sleeping Persephone, wearing a wreath in her hair. Considered by the Greeks so beautiful they were named after 'a celebrated Youth of the same name' who fell in love with his own reflection, many legends told of their uses and power.

Although certain species grew wild around the Mediterranean, cultivated daffodils and narcissi, also called 'Daffadowndyllyes', were not recorded until the 16th-century herbals. Parkinson knew seventy-eight different species. In the 19th century, experiments in hybridizing plants resulted in a growing and continuing interest in daffodil-raising, now one of our most popular flowers.

PSEUDONARCISSUS

NOW TO CAUSE YOU TO UNDERSTAND the difference betweene a true Daffodil and a false, is this: it consisteth only in the flower (when as in all other parts they cannot bee distinguished) and chiefly in the middle cup or chalice; for that we doe in a manner onely account those to bee *Pseudonarcissus*, bastard Daffodils, whose middle cup is altogether as long, and sometimes a little longer than the outer leaves that doe encompasse it, so that it seemeth rather like a trunke or long nose than a cup or chalice, such as almost all the *Narcissi*, or true Daffodils have.

PARADISI IN SOLE PARADISUS TERRESTRIS, JOHN PARKINSON, 1629

DAFFODILS AND NARCISSI

DOG'S TOOTH VIOLET, NARCISSI

OF NARCISSUS

A NARCISSUS WITH FLOWER WHITE throughout including the centre, is here described; the leaves of which are oblong and less green, the stem indeed bears four or more flowers, not so large as the flowers of the remaining Narcissus, white throughout, with a small and short cup of the same colour. It is found in many places in Spain.

The Narcissus which follows is found nowhere except in gardens, and usually appears later, namely in the month of May, having tall leaves and a stem shorter than the leaves, which bears a rather large flower, with six broad keeled white petals displayed in the form of a star, the centre of which, in place of a cup, six other smaller petals occupy, likewise white but showing somewhat of a yellowish colour scattered here and there; some stamens nevertheless adorn the centre.

HORTUS FLORIDUS, CRISPIN VAN DE PASSE. 1614

OF THE DENS CANINUS, OR DOGG TOOTH'D VIOLET

THIS PLANT HATH A SHORT BROAD GREENE LEAFE, much bespotted with a red colour, like the Orchises. They shew themselves usually in January and are ever two in number, and quickly lye along on the earth. The roote is a small long bulbe, commonly bending crooked towards the top. The flower is but one on the stalke, and is very like in shape to a little Lilly, or rather a Martagon, because the flowers hang downe, and turne a little backe, and have long seeds on chives, and a pointell. The seed is yellowish and small.

There are but two sorts that I have seene, which are the white flower'd, whose green leaves are narrower and longer than the others are, and the light purple or flesh colour. Both flower in March. They love a rich earth and a warme place, and endure not to bee long out of the ground.

THE GARDEN BOOK OF SIR THOMAS HANMER, 1659

VERE nouo redeunt florentia germina plantis,
Et monstrant qualis copia melsis erit.

Elysios campos, & suaues Veris honores,
Ingeniosa novum linea pingit opus.
Quam nos grata manent venturo secula sedo,
Quando sepulcrali mortuus exit humo.

Narcissus Sylvestris Hispanicus maximus luteus.
Narcissus
Narcissus Montanus Sylvestris iuncifolius amplo calice.
Narcissus Hispanicus. minor flore luteo.

BLOSSOMING BUDS *return to plants at the beginning of spring*
To show how good the harvest will be.

A skilful hand paints a new work
In the Elysian fields and glories of spring.
How pleasing for the generations to follow us
That the dead are risen from their earthen tombs.

HORTI ITZTEINENSIS

TO DAFFODILS

FAIR DAFFODILS, WE WEEP TO SEE
You haste away so soon:
As yet the early-rising sun
Has not attain'd his noon.
Stay, stay
Until the lasting day
Has run
But to the evensong;
And, having pray'd together, we
Will go with you along.

We have short time to stay, as you,
We have as short a spring;
As quick a growth to meet decay,
As you, or anything.
We die
As your hours do, and dry
Away
Like to the summer's rain;
Or as the pearly of morning's dew,
Ne'er to be found again.

ROBERT HERRICK (1591–1674)

DAFFODILS AND NARCISSI

OF GARDENS

GOD ALMIGHTY FIRST PLANTED A GARDEN; and indeed it is the purest of human pleasures. It is the greatest refreshment to the spirits of man; without which buildings and palaces are but gross handyworks. And a man shall ever see, that, when ages grow to civility and elegancy, men come to build stately, sooner than to garden finely: as if gardening were the greater perfection.

I do hold it, in the royal ordering of gardens there ought to be gardens for all the months in the year; in which, severally, things of beauty may be then in season. For December and January, and the latter part of November, you must take such things as are green all winter; holly, ivy, bays, juniper, cypress-trees, yews, pine-apple trees, fir-trees, rosemary, lavender, periwinkle the white, the purple, and the blue; germander, flags, orange-trees, limon-trees, and myrtles, if they be stoved; and sweet marjoram warm set.

There followeth, for the latter part of January and February, the mezerion-tree, which then blossoms, crocus vernus, both the yellow and the gray; primroses, anemonies, the early tulippa, hyacinthus orientalis, chamairis, fritellaria.

For March there come violets, specially the single blue, which are the earliest; the yellow daffodil, the daisy, the almond-tree in blossom, the peach-tree in blossom, the cornelian-tree in blossom, sweet briar.

In April follow the double white violet, the wallflower, the stock gilliflower, the cowslip, flowers-de-lice, and lilies of all natures; rosemary-flowers, the tulippa, the double piony, the pale daffadil, the french honeysuckle, the cherry-tree in blossom, the damascen and plum-trees in blossom, the white thorn in leaf, the lelac tree.

In May and June come pinks of all sorts, specially the blush-pink; roses of all kinds, except the musk, which comes later; honeysuckles, strawberries, bugloss, columbine, the french marigold, flos africanus, cherry-tree in fruit, ribies, figs in fruit, rasps, vine-flowers, lavender in flowers, the sweet satyrion with the white flower, herba muscaria, lilium convallium, the apple-tree in blossom.

In July come gilliflowers of all varieties, musk-roses; the lime-tree in blossom; early pears and plums in fruit, jennetins, codlins.

In August come plums of all sorts in fruit, pears, apricocks, barberries, filberds, must-melons, monks-hoods of all colours.

In September come grapes, apples, poppies of all colours, peaches, melo-cotones, nectarins, corn-elians, wardens, quinces.

In October, and the beginning of November, come services, medlars, bullaces; roses cut or removed to come late, holyoaks, and such like. These particulars are for the climate of London: but my meaning is perceived, that you may have *ver perpetuum*, as the place affords.

ESSAYS XLVI. OF GARDENS, FRANCES BACON. 1612.

A FRITILLARY, ANEMONES, DAFFODILS AND NARCISSI

From Hortus Floridus. Crispin van de Passe. 1614

THE PRIMROSE

Ask me why I send you here
This sweet Infanta of the year?
Ask me why I send to you
This primrose, thus bepearl'd with dew:
I will whisper to your ears: -
The sweets of love are mix'd with tears.

Ask me why this flower does show
So yellow-green, and sickly too?
Ask me why the stalk is weak
And bending (yet it doth not break)?
I will answer: - These discover
What fainting hopes are in a lover.

Robert Herrick (1591-1674)

THE PRIMULA

THE GENUS PRIMULA covers over five hundred species, many of them wild, as primroses and cowslips used to grow in profusion before the demands of 20th-century living and modern farming methods reduced their numbers. A bank of wild primroses is still one of nature's loveliest sights, as many poets throughout the ages remind us.

The probable derivation for the names primrose and primula are from the Italian *primaverola*, meaning the first flowers of spring, *fior di primavera*. In its earliest form it appears as Prymerolles. The plant had medicinal properties, useful for arthritic 'pains in the ioynts' and the flowers were eaten in 'sallets', the leaves used to salve wounds.

The pale primrose so happy in the wild is seldom happy in a garden, but garden versions were cultivated and known in Europe as English flowers, for English gardeners were thought best at frequent transplanting in almost all seasons. Coloured primroses seem hardly to have been recorded until the mid-17th century, when varieties were introduced from the East. Red, purple or yellow primroses grew in the Caucasus, Northern Persia and Greece before becoming prized in western gardens.

The wild cowslip, primula *veris*, is probably an ancestor of the polyanthus, primula *variabilis*. The polyanthus is the result of experiments at the Botanic Gardens of Oxford and Leyden in the late 17th century, crossing primroses and cowslips. These are recorded in lists of plants grown in monastic gardens in the middle ages. By the late 18th century these were 'one of the noted prize flowers among florists, many of whom are remarkably industrious in raising a considerable number of different sorts'. The polyanthus was developed by specialist 'flower-fanciers' in Cheshire and Lancashire, where the number of varieties surpassed even those grown in Holland. Popularity reached a peak about 1840, with fine examples such as the gold and silver-laced varieties, in darker colours outlined in white or yellow.

The most fashionable primula was undoubtedly the *auricula*, which, although recorded earlier, was developed and adapted in the 18th century, becoming even more popular in the 19th century. Originally an Alpine flower, known to the Romans, it is thought the first auriculas were brought to England by Huguenot refugees in the late 16th century. Gerard records several varieties in 1597, and Parkinson, who grew twenty or more kinds, including some striped varieties, records how 'being many set together upon a stalke, doe seeme every one of them to bee a Nosegay alone of it self'. The name by which Parkinson refers to the plants, Bear's Ears, *Auricula ursi*, refers to the shape of their leaves. Sir John Hanmer names forty varieties, some of whose names conjure up vividly colourful pictures 'Mistris Buggs her fine purple...'

By the mid-18th century they were cultivated as pot-plants, protected and with elaborate backgrounds to display them in full bloom. Grander names such as Marvel of the World replaced Mistress Buggs. In the 19th century, auricula societies were formed and exhibitions held, but although still popular in the north, growers around London were pushed further out by the 'enlargement of our London Babel.'

In the late 19th and early 20th century, many beautiful Asiatic primulas have been introduced from expeditions further east, to India, Nepal, China and Japan, continuing time-honoured methods of exchanges of knowledge.

FRITILLARIA.

FRITILLARIA. ab abaco in quo Scacorum lusus exercetur, quem fritillum dici existimant, nomen habet: alijs Meleagris à Meleagridis. avis plumis, quali non coloris specie. tamen varietate, & dispositione, & macularum magnitudine. refert ....

Fritillaria Præcox purpurea variegata.

Fritillaria Pyrenea atropurpurea.

Hyacinthus stellatus cineracei coloris ....

Fritillaria alba.

Botroitos flore cæruleo ....

A GARDEN OF DELIGHT

HAVING THUS FORMED OUT A GARDEN, and divided it into his fit and due proportion, with all the gracefull knots, arbours, walkes &c likewise what is fit to keepe it in the same comely order, is appointed unto it, both for the borders of the squares, and for the knots and beds themselves; let us now come and furnish the inward parts with those fine flowers (being strangers unto us, and giving the beauty and bravery of their colours so early before many of our owne bred flowers, the more to entice us to their delight) are most beseeming it; and namely, with Daffodils, Fritillarias, Jacinthes, Saffron-flowers, Lillies, Flower-deluces, Tulipas, Anemones, French Cowslips, or Beares eares, and a number of such other flowers, very beautifull, delightfull, and pleasant, hereafter described in full, whereof although many have little sweet scent to commend them, yet their earlinesse and exceeding great beautie and varietie doth so farre countervaile that defect. For the most part of these Out-landish Flowers, do shew forth their beauty and colours so early in the yeare, that they seeme to make a garden of delight even in the Winter time, and doe so give their flowers one after another, that all their bravery is not fully spent.

PARADISI IN SOLE PARADISUS TERRESTRIS , JOHN PARKINSON. 1629

FRITILLARIES, SQUILL

Hyacinth, wood anemone, Star of Bethlehem, marsh marigold, a fritillary

Hyacinthus orientalis precox, flore violaceo.
Ornithogalum Neapolitanum.
Fritillaria lutea Someri, rubris maculis distincta.
Caltha palustris flore pleno Aureo.
Ranunculus hortensis flore carneo.

THE HYACINTH

ORIGINALLY FROM the eastern Mediterranean countries of Greece and Asia Minor, the hyacinth *orientalis* was introduced to European gardens after cultivation at the world's first botanic garden in Padua in 1543. The Turks were notable gardeners, and traders in the sixteenth and seventeenth centuries: trade with Holland and subsequent Dutch cultivation and popularity culminated in some two thousand varieties by the 18th century, when bulbs were much prized, being sold for as much as £100 apiece.

OF HYACINTHS, OR JACYNTHS

THERE ARE GREAT DIVERSITYES OF THESE, differing in color, greatnes, and seasons of bearing. The fairest and largest we call ORIENTALL, because they came first out of Turkey, and the Eastern countreys, whereof there are some Blew, pale and deepe, smelling sweet, and some White, all which flower betimes, and some of the same colors which flower later, amongst which the rarest is the DOWBLE WHITE, and the Flesh color, and the Ash color. And after all these come the Violet color polyanthes, single and dowble, the sweet pale Watchet, called in Italy Januarius, from a Gardiner's name, and the dowble Sky or Blew, called there Roseus, from the figure like a rose blowne, and the Rosemary color.

These flower in March or Aprill, and have their seed ripe in the end of May, and beginning of June in England. Their greene leaves come up in December and January.

After these Orientall sorts, we esteeme two smaller sorts, that is the English and the Spanish. The English are single, of WHITE, BLEW and BLUSH colors. They flower in Aprill. The Spanish are the BLEW, the RED and the DUNNE, or a sad white color. They flower in May. Besides all these there is a sort of the true Hyacinths which hath a Lilly leafe, and a strong stalke spotted with red, and large BLEW flowers. It beares in Aprill.

THE GARDEN BOOK OF SIR THOMAS HANMER, 1659

Corona Imperialis, lútea

TO THE WESTERN WIND

Sweet western wind, whose luck it is,
Made rival with the air,
To give Perenna's lip a kiss,
And fan her wanton hair.

Bring me but one, I'll promise thee,
Instead of common showers,
Thy wings shall be embalm'd by me,
And all beset with flowers.

Robert Herrick (1591–1674)

CROWN IMPERIAL

This plant was first brought from Constantinople into these Christian Countries. It flowereth most commonly in the end of March, if the weather be milde. It is of some called *Lilium Persicum*, the Persian Lily; but because wee have another, which is more usually called by that name, I had rather with Alphonsus Pancius, the Duke of Florence, his Physitian, call it *Corona Imperialis*, The Crowne Imperiall, than by any other name. This was, as it is thought, first brought from Persia unto Constantinople, and from thence, sent unto us by the meanes of divers Turkie Merchants.

Paradisi in Sole Paradisus Terrestris, John Parkinson, 1629

Tusai, or the persian lily, commonly, the double crown imperial, makes a succession of blooms. *At Idstein on 21st April 1662, this flowered on a stem five feet tall carrying 27 blooms.*

CROWN IMPERIAL

Tulips

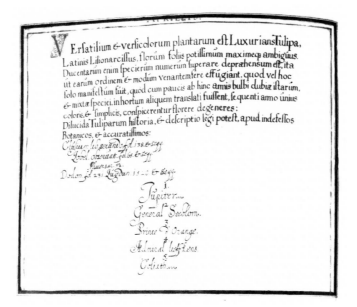

The luxuriant tulip (in Latin Lilionarcissus), is among the most varied plants in form and colour. It has been found that there exist more than two hundred different varieties: however, in order that they be shown capable of altering both their shape and way of growth this experiment was tried. After a few years in the garden, bulbs whose form was unknown but were of different varieties were transplanted into a different garden. In the following year they were perceived to bloom all in the same colour and to have changed in form.

This very clear story of the tulip and the description of the result of the experiment have been attested by the most distinguished and meticulous botanists.

HORTI ITZTEINENSIS

THE TULIP'S FIRST
FLOWERING IN EUROPE

"In this year of our lord 1559 at the beginning of April in the garden of the ingenious and learned Councillor John Henry Herwart I saw there a plant which had sprung from seed which had been procured from Byzantia, or as some say from Cappadocia. It was growing with one large reddish flower, like a red lily, having eight petals of which four are outside, and just as many within, with a pleasant smell, soothing and delicate, which soon leaves it."

DE HORTIS GERMANIAE, CONRAD GESNER

These tulips have taken their names from the following lovers of flowers:

1. *Prince de Wallis*
2. *General van Seeland*
3. *Booterman*
4. *Scipio*
5. *La plus belle de Brussele*

<small>HORTI ITZTEINENSIS</small>

OF TULIPS

OF ALL WHICH THE TULIP HATH OBTAINED and not undeservedly the preference, yielding so great a Variety, that they are not here to be enumerated, every Year producing new Flowers, nor is it all the words I can invent can convince you of the beauty of these Glories of Nature, but must refer you to the choice, your self or friend for you, can make out of that magazin of varieties that are collected by the Ingenious Florist.

Their Colours are various, from the deepest dy of any other Flowers to the purest White, intermixt with the brightest Yellow, transcendent Scarlet, grave Purple and many other compounds of these inclining to the Blew and Green.

Their Season of Blowing continues long, the Praecoces or early Tulips, beginning some of them to blow at the Vernal Equinox, the Medias which are the prime, continue all April and sometimes the half of May, till the end whereof the Serotines or late Flowering Tulips continue.

When the principal of them display their Colours in the heat of the day there is not a more Glorious sight in Nature nor is it to be imitated by Art, no Limmer nor Painter dare pretend to so great a skill: but as all things else that are in excess are soonest apt to decline, so these that precede all others in beauty and lustre, soonest fade, not any of them continuing in its Glory above eight or ten dayes, unless the mildness of the weather or some artificial shade preserve them, nor are they succeeded by any other from the same root.

<small>SYSTEMA HORTICULTURAE, or THE ART OF GARDENING,
JOHN WOOLRIDGE, 1677</small>

TULIPS

From Hortus Floridus, Crispin van de Passe. 1614

OF TULIPS

THE GREATER TULIPAS have first been sent to us from Constantinople, and other parts of Turkie, where it is said they grow naturally wilde in the Fields, Woods, and Mountaines: as Thracia, Macedonia, Pontus, about the Euxine Sea, Cappadocia, Buthynia, and about Tripolis and Aleppo in Syria also: the lesser have come from severall places, as their names doe descipher it out unto us; as Armenia, Persia, Candye, Portugall, Spaine, Italy and France. They are all made Denizens in our Gardens, where they yeeld us more delight, and more encrease for their proportion, by reason of the culture, than they did unto their owne naturals.

PARADISI IN SOLE PARADISUS TERRESTRIS.
JOHN PARKINSON. 1629

VARIETY OF TULIPS

S O GREAT IS THE VARIETY OF TULIPS year by year as very often to mock or surpass the desires of the growers, and so it is very difficult even for one who is expert to express them in words.

But this first Tulip can rightly be called *flammea*, its whole flower is resplendent, decorated with flames of sulphur-yellow and scarlet colour: although at the base it is scarcely yellow, at the tops of its petals it is brilliant with flames of a deep purple colour. The flower of the second by no means yields to its companion in elegance, it is less yellow but stands out more brightly with rays of a whitish colour and observers reluctantly withdraw their eyes from it.

The plant of *Tulipa Persica* sent by the illustrious Caccinus to the famous Clusius flowered along with the early Tulips: and put forth in the year 1607 a stem a foot long, quite slender, provided with four leaves, not very broad, and keeled........ The petals of our flower of this are nearly all sharp-pointed and seem to differ but little among themselves in form.

The second, first brought from Crete as is believed, hence its name, is provided with leaves broader than a lily, and bears also an open flower, in the shape of a lily, with a very elegant mixture of white and purple colour, also remarkable for a saffron-yellow base and black stamens, a not unpleasing spectacle.

HORTUS FLORIDUS, CRISPIN VAN DE PASSE, 1614

TULIPOMANIA

Although the tulip was first cultivated as a garden flower in Turkey, it also grew wild there and a description from Busbecq, Ambassador from the court of Emperor Ferdinand I to Suleiman the Magnificent, remains the first documentary evidence of tulips growing wild. In 1554, on his way from Adrianople to Constantinople, Augerius de Busbecq noticed 'an abundance of flowers everywhere - narcissus, hyacinths, and those which the Turks call *tulipam* - much to our astonishment, because it was almost mid-winter, a season unfriendly to flowers. Greece abounds in narcissus and hyacinths remarkable for their fragrance, which is so strong as to hurt those not used to it; the *tulipam*, however, have little or no smell, but are admired for the beauty and variety of their colours. The Turks pay great attention to the cultivation of flowers. I received several presents of these flowers, which cost me not a little.'

It is probable that Busbecq misunderstood his interpreter, comparing the shape of the petals to that of a turban *dulban*, or in Persian *toliban* - as the word actually used for the flower was *lale*. Nonetheless, the name was handed down, as were seeds which he brought back to Vienna, and probably also the bulbs.

The fame of the tulip spread quickly, descriptions survive of its growth in Germany and soon cargoes of bulbs were travelling regularly from Constantinople.

The tulip reached Holland from Flanders and in about 1578 reached England. The great 17th-century gardening writers, such as Gerard and Parkinson sang the praises of the tulip, whose fame for a time surpassed that of the daffodil and even the rose. Poets too were moved by the flower's short-lived beauty.

More extraordinary to us now than the romance seen in this flower, was the *Tulipomania* which reached its height between the years 1634 and 1637 in Holland. The bulbs that first came from Turkey were not the wild kind, but the cultivated. These self-cultivated tulips, known as 'breeders' have a strange habit of breaking up into variegated forms, from which they rarely revert. Thus, unpredictability of colour and pattern of stripes became a freak on which gamblers could bet and place their chances. 'If a change in a tulip is effected . . . soon it gets talked about. Everyone is anxious to see it. If it is a new flower, each one gives his opinion.'

The enthusiasm of amateurs had forced the prices of bulbs up to ridiculous amounts: soon everyone was growing bulbs. Together with the actual growing went speculation, gambling huge amounts to invest in the craze. Soon every town had a club for tulip trading. Sales took place between June, when the bulbs were lifted, and September, when they should be replanted.

For one 'Viceroy' bulb it was recorded that the following goods were exchanged: 2 loads of wheat; 4 loads of rye; 4 fat oxen; 8 fat pigs; 12 fat sheep; 2 hogsheads of wine; 4 barrels of 8-florin beer; 2 barrels of butter; 1,000 lb. of cheese; a complete bed; a suit of clothes and a silver beaker - the whole valued at 2,500 florins.

TULIP

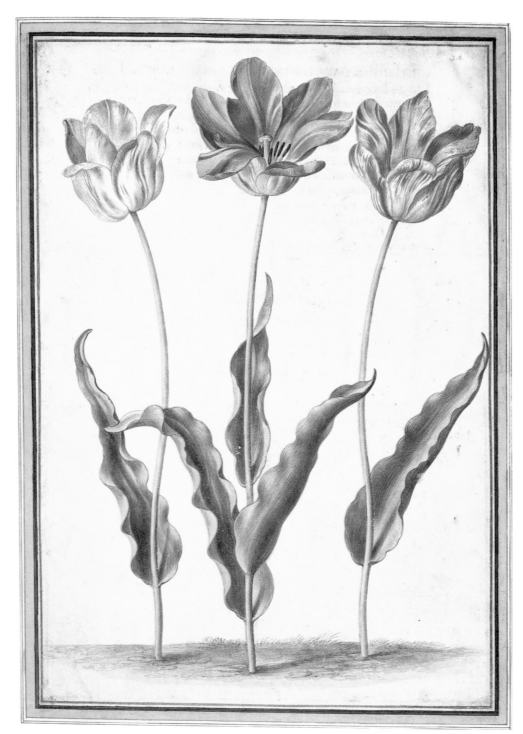

TULIPS

THE TULIP

THE TULIP WAS INTRODUCED to England about 1578, as in 1582 the nephew of the explorer Hakluyt recorded that 'divers kinds of flowers called Tulipas' had been brought 'from Vienna in Austria . . . by an excellent man called M. Carolus Clusius'.

The most highly regarded were the striped varieties, described by John Rea as 'Striped, feathered, garded or variously marbled'. Late 18th century nursery catalogues listed as many as 665 different varieties.

A GARDEN
WRITTEN AFTER THE CIVIL WARS

SEE HOW THE FLOWERS, AS AT PARADE,
Under their colours stand display'd:
Each regiment in order grows,
That of the tulip, pink, and rose.
But when the vigilant patrol
Of stars walks round about the pole,
Their leaves, that to the stalks are curl'd,
Seem to their staves the ensigns furl'd.
Then in some flower's beloved hut
Each bee, as sentinel, is shut,
And sleeps so too; but if once stirr'd,
She runs you through, nor asks the word.
  O thou, that dear and happy Isle,
The garden of the world erewhile,

Thou Paradise of the four seas
Which Heaven planted us to please,
But, to exclude the world, did guard
With wat'ry, if not flaming, sword;
What luckless apple did we taste
To make us mortal and thee waste!
Unhappy! shall we never more
That sweet militia restore,
When gardens only had their towers,
And all the garrisons were flowers;
When roses only arms might bear,
And men did rosy garlands wear?

ANDREW MARVELL (1621-78)

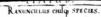

> *RANUNCULUS* and wild parsley belong to the fields: ranunculus, after the manner of frogs, lies hidden in moist paths and shady borders, or else frogs are frequently found between its stems. Apium with its leaves resembles wild parsley. Caspar Bauhin.
>
> HORTI ITZTEINENSIS

literal Latin translation means a little frog. The Latin here is an untranslatable pun. Apium can also mean of bees, or the garlands of parsley worn by victors in the ancient literature of Virgil or Horace : Pliny 19 explains.

OF RANUNCULES

THE GLANDULOUS KIND OF RANUNCULUS (for there are others) have their rootes consisting of very small knobs, like graines of wheate, and are usually called in Latine *Ranunculi Asiatici*, Ranunculus of Asia, and French Ranuncules de Tripoly, of Tripoly, a towne in Barbary. The stalkes are many, long and hairy as the leaves also are, which are fatt and thicke, and devided commonly into three divisions, of a yellowish greene colour. There are single and dowble sorts, both beautifull.

THE GARDEN BOOK OF SIR THOMAS HANMER, 1659

RANUNCULUS

TRADITION HAS IT that the Asiatic Ranunculus or Persian King-cup was brought home to Europe from the Crusades by King Louis XI of France. Another story tells of the flower seen growing wild in Turkey by a court Vizier, who introduced the plant to the Sultan's gardens.

ANEMONES, GARDEN RANUNCULUS

FROM HORTUS FLORIDUS, CRISPIN VAN DE PASSE, 1614

ASIATIC RANUNCULUS

Batrachium is called in Latin *Ranunculus* because it delights in places and brinks which are perchance damp. But here two *Asiatic Ranunculi* are figured, the one with a simple, the other with a twin double flower; having at the base three or four leaves, supported by long stalks, cut along the edges, and divided into three segments, rather pale green: between these springs forth the stem quite strong, provided with leaves which are divided into thinner and more numerous segments; on the top of the stalk of the first species a fairly large flower is seated, consisting of six or more petals in a single series, of a crimson colour throughout, but on the outside rather deeply, on the inside more brightly reddish; the centre of the flower is filled by a rather large and dark head.

The double flower of the second *Ranunculus* of the same colour, is so remarkable with its multiplicity of petals, that it is found far to exceed the hundredth number of petals, and what is surprising, puts forth from the centre of the flower another thin stalk which is fruitful with a similar but smaller floret.

HORTUS FLORIDUS, CRISPIN VAN DE PASSE, 1614

RANUNCULUS

Aʟᴛʜᴏᴜɢʜ ᴛʜᴇ ꜰɪᴇʟᴅ ʙᴜᴛᴛᴇʀᴄᴜᴘ is the most common flower we know today of the ranunculus family, in earlier days the cultivated ranunculus was one of the most popular flowers to be found in a garden.

One of the plants the Huguenots are supposed to have brought over with them in the late 16th century was *Ranunculus aconitifolius*, which might account for its name, Fair Maids of France. *Ranunculus acris* was found to grow near Shakespeare's Globe Theatre, and another form of *Ranunculus repens* was known by Gerard as Bachelor's Buttons.

Ranunculus Asiaticus was possibly distributed from roots procured from the Sultan of Turkey's garden, where a Vizier had introduced it after finding it growing wild in the fields. The Sultan's courtiers gave roots to interested gardeners: by the 16th century Turkey was exporting corms to Europe.

Gerard records how the corms were imported from Turkey to Europe in the 16th century, not always surviving the long journey, and arriving dry as ginger, 'notwithstanding Clusius saith he received a plant fresh and greene, which a domesticall theefe stole foorth of his garden...'

However, once the flower was raised from seed instead of relying on imported corms, it grew in variety and popularity, engaging serious attention by the end of the 17th century. 'Among all the Flowers that adorn a Garden, the Ranunculus is one of the best esteem'd, and if it were but Odoriferous, as it is not, it would be a masterpiece of Nature' wrote Liger in 1706.

The most prized were the white or yellow flowers with red stripes, or white backed with rose, followed by the white with brownish red and yellow, and then the double red was least valued. At one stage, there was such variety of colour that it was in competition with the carnation.

The popularity rose to the heights of nearly 800 named kinds in a catalogue of 1792, but by 1820 the number had dwindled to half these. By the mid-19th century it was described as a 'neglected flower' and it is possible that difficulty of cultivation was a cause of its decline.

AMARYLLIS, ANEMONE

Lilio Narcissus Hemerocalli disfacie. fiue Narcissus Mathioli.

IN THE PARTERRE AND FLOWER GARDEN: MARCH

Plant some anemony roots to bear late, and successively; especially in and about London, where the smoak is any thing tolerable; and if the season be very dry, water them well once in two or three days, as likewise Ranunculus's. Fibrous roots may be transplanted about the middle of this moneth, such as Hepaticas, Primroses, Auriculas, Cammomile, Narcissus tuberose, Matricaria, Gentianella, Hellebore and other summer flowers; set Leucoium; slip the Keris or Wallflower; and towards the end, Lupines, Convolvulus's, spanish, or ordinary Jasmine.

Kalendarium Hortense : or the Gard'ner's Almanac.
John Evelyn, 1659

IN THE PARTERRE AND FLOWER GARDEN: APRIL

Water anemones, Ranunculus's, and Plants in Pots and Cases once in two or three days, if drouth require it. But carefully protect from violent storms of Rain, Hail and the parching darts of the Sun, your pennach'd Tulips, Ranunculus's, Anemonies, Auricula's, covering them with mattrasses supported on cradles of hoops, which have now in readiness.

Kalendarium Hortense : or the Gard'ner's Almanac John Evelyn, 1659

Floriferis oculis abundat exigua radix Anemones, ut omnium
voluptati oculorum quàm maximè prospiciat. Sunt, qui anemonen Phenion vocent: alii Adonidis ab apro interempti florem appellant: alii
Veneris Adonidem lugentis lacrymas in eum florem concrevisse debla-
terant, innocentissimi risum floris impurà fabulæ tragico luctu funest-
antes: alii denique vim Græci nominis interpretati florem venti nominant,
quia non sine vento aperitur.

*T*HE TINY STEM OF THE ANEMONE *abounds in flowery buds,
presenting a most pleasing sight for all eyes that may gaze upon it.
There are those who call the anemone "Phenion"; others call it the
flower of Adonis, who was killed by a boar; others maintain that the
tears of Venus as she wept for Adonis hardened into that flower,
polluting the smile of a totally innocent flower with the tragic grief of
a shameful story. Finally, others, following the etymology of the
Greek name, call it the flower of the wind, because it opens only when
the wind is blowing.*

HORTI ITZTEINENSIS

O F A N E M O N E S

MANY FINE-COLOUR'D STARRS have beene rais'd
from the seed of the single Hard leav'd kinds...but
the PAVO Maior and the other stript ones come from
beyond sea.

I know not any Flower soe nice and hard to bee
humour'd in its culture as these starr Anemones.
The single will blow well in any good mold and
indifferent ayr, but the Dowble ones or starrs,
though the rootes will live well enough abroad all
wynter, yet the flowers will bee large and well
colour'd but in few places, like the dowble yellow
rose. The best way to treat them is to bestow on them
very good rich mold, somwhat moist with old
consum'd dung, to let them bee a very short tyme

out of the ground, to water them often, and let them
stand warme, but not too much expos'd to the sun.

When you remove them let it bee in the end of
May or June, and plant them as soone againe as you
can, but the seldomer remov'd the better.

Sow the seed of the dowble flowers or starrs, if
you can get it, if not, of the single sorts, in potts or
tubbs in August, in very fine sifted earth, very thin,
and cover it as lightly as may bee, and let them stand
in the shade till wynter,unless you give them the
morning sun somtymes.

THE GARDEN BOOK OF SIR THOMAS HANMER, 1659

ANEMONES

Irises

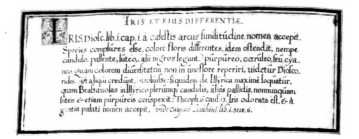

*T*HE IRIS ACCORDING TO DIOSCORIDES *(Book 1, Chapter 1) took its name from its resemblance to a rainbow. The same authority shows that there are several species, differing according to the colour of the flower, viz. pure white, a pale yellow, golden yellow, purple (others say 'black') sky-blue or dark blue. Dioscorides seems not to have preferred this diversity of colour in a single flower, since he talks most about the Illyrian iris which Brassauolas saw in Illyria, mostly pure white, others pale, sometimes golden-yellow and even purple-red. Theophrastus 6. Topic 13 describes it thus " The iris is scented and named on account of the palate." Caspar Bauhin lib 1 sect.6*

HORTI ITZTEINENSIS

THE FLAGGE OR FLOWERDELUCE

THE GREAT TURKIE FLOWERDELUCE

*T*HE GREAT TURKIE FLOWERDELUCE, hath divers heads of long and broad fresh greene leaves. The flower is of the colour almost of a Snakes skinne, it is so diversely spotted; for the three lower falling leaves are very large, of a deepe or darke purple colour, almost blacke, full of grayish spots, strakes, and lines through the whole leaves, which leaves being laid in water, will colour the water into a Violet colour, but if a litle Allome be put therein, and then wrung or pressed, and the juice of these leaves dryed in the shadow, will give a colour almost as depe as Indico, and may serve for shawdowes for limming excellent well: the flower hath no sent that can be perceived, but is onely commendable for the beauty and rarity thereof.

THE YELLOW FLOWERDELUCE OF TRIPOLY

*T*HIS FLOWERDELUCE I place in the forefront of the narrow leafed Flowerdeluces. It beareth leaves a yard long, or not much lesse, and an inch broad, of a sad greene colour, but not shining: the stalke riseth up to be foure or five foote high, being strong and round, but not very great, bearing at the topp two or three long and narrow gold yellow flowers, of the fashion of the bulbous Flowerdeluces.

Both the rootes and the flowers of the great Flowerdeluces, are of great use for the purging and cleansing of many inward, as well as outward diseases, as all Authors in Physicke doe record.

PARADISI IN SOLE PARADISUS TERRESTRIS,
JOHN PARKINSON, 1629

THE IRIS

REPRESENTED IN EGYPTIAN TOMB PAINTINGS in the temple at Karnak, the iris is one of the oldest cultivated plants. It was a symbol of eloquence, used to adorn statues of the Sphinx. The iris was named after the rainbow because of the wide spectrum of its colouring. Amongst other strange medicinal uses, it was believed to be a cure for dropsy. shortness of breath, coughs and bruises. Iris *germanica* is known to have grown in Europe in the ninth century, according to Walafrid Strabo, the Abbot of Reichenau. Iris *fiorentina* supplied the sweet-scented 'orris-root' used to make toilet preparations.

THOUGHTS IN A GARDEN

HOW VAINLY MEN THEMSELVES AMAZE
To win the palm, the oak, or bays,
And their uncessant labours see
Crown'd from some single herb or tree,
Whose short and narrow-verged shade
Does prudently their toils upbraid;
While all the flowers and trees do close
To weave the garlands of repose!

Fair Quiet, have I found thee here,
And Innocence thy sister dear?
Mistaken long, I sought you then
In busy companies of men:
Your sacred plants, if here below,
Only among the plants will grow:
Society is all but rude
To this delicious solitude...........

ANDREW MARVELL (1621-78)

IRISES

IRISES

Iris Bulbosa angustifolia flore vario.
Iris Florentina.
Iris Lusitanica.
Narcissus Indicus.

OF BULBOUS IRISES

THERE ARE TWO SORTS of BULBOUS IRISES, the GREAT or LATIFOLIAS, because they have broader leaves than the other, and are stronger plants.
The LESSER or ANGUSTIFOLIAS, after the Latine word, because they have narrower greene leaves, and have smaller rootes and flowers than the former.

Of the GREAT SORT wee have but a few in comparison of the other, and they are generally by writers called English irises, as if they were most of them naturall to our country, but I have not knowne any of them grow wild or naturally in England as some of the Flag-leav'd doe.

GREAT BULBOUS IRISES

THESE FOLLOWING are all the varietyes I have seene:

CLUSIUS his FIRST IRIS, soe called from him that described it first and because hee treats of it first in his booke. It is commonly of a pale BLEW colour, but sometimes WHITE is to bee found.

It is also called IRIS LUSITANICA LATIFOLIA, the broad leav'd Portugall Iris. It flowers first of any Iris in the Spring, in January commonly.

The PERSIAN Iris, whose falls or falling leaves are of a shining MURREY or deepe purple, like velvet, and the standards of a very pale WATCHET. It flowers betimes in February.

All Bulbous Irises have their standards much lesse than their falling leaves, and the Tuberous the contrary ever.

They love a reasonable loose mold, somewhat sandy, and rot presently if new dung come to the rootes.

It is better to let them stand two or three yeares than to take them up yearly, and it is not good to keepe them long out of the earth, but they may without great hurt bee kept as long a Tulipes unsett. The tyme to take them up is when the stalkes are well wither'd, and to replant them any tyme from Michelmas or beginning of September to Christmas, or very neare.

The SEED is to bee sowed and ordered as Tulipe seed, that of the lesser sorte of bulbous Irises produces often new kinds, but the striping comes commonly with age, as it does to Tulipes.

In fower years your seed will bring flowers.

There needs no more to bee sayd of them, but that they are all hardy enough, prospering better abroad in the full earth with us than in potts, and in the shade than too hot a sun.

They all encrease exceedingly in offsetts, if they like the ground.

THE GARDEN BOOK OF SIR THOMAS HANMER, 1659

AQUILEIA ET EIUS DIFFERENTIÆ.

Hæc diversorum colorem reperitur, cærúleo, candido, incarnato, rúbro, variegato ex cærúleo & púrpúreo: candido, nonnúllis velú. tis litúris cerúleis aspersis.____

COLUMBINE

AQUILEGIA *VULGARIS* or columbine has long been a favourite in cottage gardens. Known popularly as 'granny-bonnets' the Latin name derives from *aquila* meaning an eagle, whereas the English name columbine comes from *columba*, a dove. Both these bird references describe the shape of the flower, described as another bird in Tournefort's *Herbal* as being 'composed of plain Petals intermixed with others that are hollow and horned, so that they imitate a Pidgeon with expanded Wings.'

Columbines were used in the 14th century as remedies for pestilence but fell out of favour as were also related to poisonous plants. It has featured in literature from Chaucer's day to the evocative country poetry of John Clare, who describes a garden of columbines:

The Columbine, stone-blue, or deep night-brown,
Their honey-comb-like flowers hanging down...

OF COLUMBINES

THE DOUBLE COLUMBINE, DOUBLE INVERTED COLUMBINE, ROSE COLUMBINE, AND DEGENERATE COLUMBINE

COSTAEUS DOTH CALL THIS PLANT *Pothos* of Theophrastus, which Gaza translateth Desiderium. We generally (I thinke) throughout the whole Countrey, Columbines.

Some in Spaine, as Camerarius saith, use to eate a peece of the roote hereof fasting, many dayes together, to helpe them that are troubled with the stone in the kindneyes. Others use the decoction, of both herbe and roote in wine, with a little Ambargrise. Clusius writeth from the experience of Franciscus Rapard, a chiefe Physician of Bruges in Flanders, that the seede beaten and drunke is effectuall to women in travell of childe.

PARADISI IN SOLE PARADISUS TERRESTRIS, JOHN PARKINSON, 1629

Columbines

PÆONIA.

PÆONIA vetuſtiſsima inventū eſt, nomenɋ authoris retinet, quam quidam Pentorobon appellant, alij Glycyſiden. Dicta Pæonia, à Medico Pæone, qui ea Plutonem ab Hercule vulneratūm. Homero Odyſſ.s. fingente, curaſſe perhibetur.

Pæonia mas maior flore, incarnato, Floris amplitudine reliquas ſuperat:

THE PEONY HAS LONG BEEN KNOWN and retains the name of its discoverer. (Pliny Book 27 and 25) Some call it Pentorobon, others Glycysiden. The peony is called after the doctor Paeon who is believed to have healed Pluto after he had been wounded by Hercules (according to Homer, Odyssey 5).

The male peony is larger when its flowers have come into bloom, surpassing the other flowers.

HORTI ITZTEINENSIS

THE PEONY

THE SINGLE BLUSH PEONY; THE DOUBLE BLUSH PEONY; AND THE SINGLE RED PEONY OF CONSTANTINOPLE

ALL THESE PEONIES have been sent or brought from divers parts beyond the Seas; they are endenized in our Gardens, where wee cherish them for the beauty and delight of their goodly flowers, as well as for their Physicall vertues.

The male Peony roote is farre above all the rest a most singular approved remedy for all Epilepticall diseases, in English, The falling sicknesses (and more especially the greene roote than the dry) if the disease be not too inveterate, to be boyled and drunke, as also to hang about the neckes of the younger sort that are troubled herewith, as I have found it sufficiently experimented on many by divers.

PARADISI IN SOLE PARADISUS TERRESTRIS, JOHN PARKINSON, 1629

Peony

FROM HORTUS FLORIDUS, CRISPIN VAN DE PASSE, 1614

THE GREAT FEMALE PAEONE

IT WAS CALLED *Paeonia* from Paeon its discoverer; and *Glycisida* from the Grecian authors because it was seen to have seeds similar to those of a pomegranate. The stems of the female paeony, unlike those of the male, are but little or not at all reddened; the leaves, down-drooping as in *hipposelinion* (which Theophrastus had called *Smyrnion*), for the most part not only divided, but also strikingly narrower than in the male paeony, greener on the upper surfaces, and waxing paler underneath. The flowers are very large, brightly flaming with crimson, luxuriant in the number of their petals, as many as two hundred being enclosed within the orbit of each flower. The dark, rounded seeds are in husks similar to those of the almond; some of which seeds are resplendent with a scarlet colour, but less so than in the male paeony. Many glandulous roots descend from one centre, similar to the roots of the true asphodel, but much thicker and longer; from which often are sent forth two or three rootlets, always of the same shape. It flowers in the month of May, an ornament of gardens.

HORTUS FLORIDUS, CRISPIN VAN DE PASSE, 1614

PAEONIA – PEONIE

THERE ARE TWO PRINCIPALL KINDES OF PEONIE, that is to say, the Male and the Female. The Male Peonie riseth up with many brownish stalkes, whereon doe grow winged leaves, that is, many faire greene and sometimes reddish leaves, one set against another upon a stalke, without any particular division in the leafe at all: the flowers stand at the toppes of the stalkes, consisting of five or six broade leaves, of a faire purplish red colour. The Female Peonie hath many stalkes, with more store of leaves on them than the Male kinde hath, the leaves also are not so large. The flowers are of a strong heady sent, most usually smaller than the male, and of a more purple tending to a murrey colour.

THE DOUBLE RED PEONIE

THIS DOUBLE PEONIE as well as the former single, is so frequent in everie Garden of note, through every Countrey, that it is almost labour in vaine to describe it: but yet because I use not to passe over any plant so slightly, I will set down the description briefly. The flowers at the tops of the stalkes are very large, thicke and double (no flower that I know so faire, great, and double: but not abiding blowne about eight or ten daies).

PARADISI IN SOLE PARADISUS TERRESTRIS, JOHN PARKINSON, 1629

PAEONIA

THE PEONY WAS FROM TIME IMMEMORIAL one of China's most ancient and symbolic plants, but its European history dates back to the ancient Greeks. Named after the physician, Paeon, who healed the wounds of the gods, it was believed to have toning properties in its roots. The ancients imbued it with supernatural powers, rather like the mandrake root. They believed it should be gathered at dead of night, for fear of woodpeckers pecking out the eyes, and uprooted by a dog tied to it by a string as the groan of the plant leaving the ground was fatal to any who heard it.

The seeds and roots of both peony *mascula* and *officinalis* were used as remedies, although by the 18th century were less well regarded as cures. Earlier, Culpeper is recorded as saying 'Physicians say Male Peony roots are best, but Dr. Reason told me Male Peony was best for Men, and Female Peony for Women, and he desires to be judged by his brother, Dr. Experience.'

HELLEBORINE, CRANESBILLS

GERANIUM Eiusq;Species.

Geranium à grüini capitis imagine, in summo eius cacumine visenda, nomen habet: at recentiores à Ciconiæ rostri effigie, Rostrum Ciconiæ nominant Geranium, é aliquibus Myrrhis, aliis Merthryda

Geranium sive batrachium cæruleum, vulgo Storchschnabel. Variat flore cæruleo, albo, é albo lineis cæruleis variegato: Geranium fulcum Orchis Serapias, secundum Dodonæi

*T*HE GERANIUM *takes its name from its resemblance to the head of a crane, to be seen at its topmost extremity; but more modern people call it "stork's bill" from its resemblance to the bill of a stork. The geranium, is to some "myrtis" (Pliny) and the others "merthyris" (Latin names from the Greek).*

The geranium or blue ranunculus, commonly known as cranesbill. It has varieties of sky-blue flowers, and white or white variegated with sky-blue threads.

HORTI ITZTEINENSIS

GERANIUM

*T*HE BLUE-FLOWERED GARDEN GERANIUMS or cranesbills originally grew wild as native plants. Geranium *pratense* and *sylvaticum* were northern flowers: in Iceland the flowers were used to make a blue-grey dye, and Tradescant brought home a *'geranium flore serulle'* in 1618, found near Archangel, in Russia.

The German name for the crane's-bill, *Gottesgnade*, derives from 'Odin's Favour' or 'Odin's Grace' and was commonly translated in English to Gratia Dei, although the Geranium *pratense* was also known as Crowfoot or Meadow cranesbill. The wild geranium, *Robertiana*, was known as Herb Robert, theoretically used to cure a disease in Germany known as Robert's Plague.

They were also called Bassinets, from an old French word meaning bowl-shaped flowers. The herbalist William Turner was very dubious about their healing qualities, although they were formerly believed to be good for healing wounds.

The cranesbill was always a popular plant in cottage gardens as well as in herbaceous borders. Today's fashion for wilder, meadow gardens make perfect settings for the garden geranium.

OF THE VARIOUS
KINDS OF ROSES

THERE IS NO FLOWER-BEARING TREE that yields to great variety, nor any blossoms so beautiful as the Rose, nor do they only adorn but perfume your Gardens.

Now I perceive from whence the Odours flow,
While on the Roses kinder Zephyrs Blow.
Out of the Prickly Stalk the Purple-Flower,
Springs, and commands the Vulgar to adore,
The Garden-Queen doth now herself display,
Soiling the Lustre of the rising Day.

SYSTEMA HORTICULTURAE, OR THE ART OF GARDENING,
JOHN WOOLRIDGE, 1677

GO, LOVELY ROSE

GO, LOVELY ROSE,
Tell her that wastes her time and me,
That now she knows,
When I resemble her to thee,
How sweet and fair she seems to be.

Tell her that's young,
And shuns to have her graces spied,
That hadst thou sprung
In deserts where no men abide,
Thou must have uncommended died.

Small is the worth
Of beauty from the light retired
Bid her come forth
Suffer herself to be desired,
And not blush so to be admired.

Then die, that she
The common fate of all things rare
May read in thee;
How small a part of time they share
That are so wondrous sweet and fair!

EDMUND WALLER (1606-87)

ROSA GALLICA

L. Rosa centifolia Batavica.

OF FLOWER-TREES

AFTER YOUR GARDEN, AVENUES, AND GROVES are reduced into such form as you desire, and those adorn'd so far as necessarily they ought to be, with those graceful and immortal Greens and other pleasant Trees yielding shade and delight, it then behoves you to furnish those intervals that remain, and the borders of your Walks with Flowers, the wonders of Nature for the richness and variety of their Colours, Scents, Forms, and Seasons. Amongst all which those Shrubs or Trees yielding so great a variety of those objects are most to be prized, and of these is the Rose to be preferred.

SYSTEMA HORTICULTURAE, OR THE ART OF GARDENING,
JOHN WOOLRIDGE, 1677

THE DAMASK ROSE

THE SWEETEST AND MOST USEFUL of Roses is the Damask, which in my Lord Bacon's time was by him observed not to have been in England above two years, of these Damask kinds there is one that bearest blossoms with the first, and so continues with new Blossoms until the frosts prevent it, and is therefore called the Monthly Rose, and is not inferior in smell to the Damask, and deserves a place amongst your most select plants, this seems to be the Rose that Pliny mentions to be growing in Spain that blow and Flower all the Winter.

The Damask Province Rose differs from the ordinary Damask in that only it is very double and fair but not so sweet.

SYSTEMA HORTICULTURAE, OR THE ART OF GARDENING,
JOHN WOOLRIDGE, 1677

TO THE VIRGINS, TO MAKE MUCH OF TIME

GATHER YE ROSEBUDS WHILE YE MAY,
Old Time is still a-flying:
And this same flower that smiles to-day
To-morrow will be dying.

The glorious lamp of heaven, the sun,
The higher he's a-getting,
The sooner will his race be run,
And nearer he's to setting.

That age is best which is the first,
When youth and blood are warmer;
But being spent, the worse, and worst
Times still succeed the former.

Then be not coy, but use your time,
And while ye may, go marry:
For having lost but once your prime,
You may for every tarry.

ROBERT HERRICK (1591-1674)

Roses

THE ROSE

A ROSE, AS FAIR AS EVER SAW THE NORTH,
Grew in a little garden all alone;
A sweeter flower did Nature ne'er put forth,
Nor fairer garden yet was never known:
The maidens danced about it morn and noon,
And learned bards of it their ditties made;
The nimble fairies by the pale-faced moon
Water'd the root and kiss'd her pretty shade.
But well-a-day! –the gardener careless grew;
The maids and fairies both were kept away,
And in a drought the caterpillars threw
Themselves upon the bud and every spray.
God shield the stock! If heaven send no supplies,
The fairest blossom of the garden dies.

WILLIAM BROWNE (1588-1643)

OF THE SCENT OF FLOWERS

AND BECAUSE THE BREATH OF FLOWERS is far sweeter in the air (where it comes and goes, like the warbling of music) than in the hand, therefore nothing is more fit for that delight, than to know what be the flowers and plants that do best perfume the air. Roses, damask and red, are flowers tenacious of their smells; so that you may walk by a whole row of them, and find nothing of their sweetness; yea, though it be in a morning's dew. Bays likewise yield no smell as they grow, rosemary little, nor sweet marjoram.

That which above all others yields the sweetest smell in the air is the violet, specially the white double violet, which comes twice a year, about the middle of April, and about Bartholomew-tide. Next to that is the musk-rose; then the strawberry leaves drying with a most excellent cordial smell. Then the flower of the vines: it is a little dust, like the dust of a bent, which grows upon the cluster in the first coming forth. Then sweet-briar; then wall-flowers; which are very delightful to be set under a parlour or lower chamber window. Then pinks and gilliflowers, especially the matted pink, and clove-gilliflower. Then the flowers of the lime-tree. Then the honey-suckles, so they be somewhat afar off. Of bean-flowers I speak not, because they are field-flowers.

But those which perfume the air most delightfully, not passed by as the rest, but being trodden upon and crushed, are three; that is, burnet, wild thyme, and water-mints. Therefore you are to set whole valleys of them, to have the pleasure when you walk or tread.

ESSAYS XLVI. OF GARDENS. FRANCES BACON, 1612.

Balaustia flore pleno maiore...
Melanthium seu Nigella cretica.
Gelsiminum Indicum odoratissimum.

In the Parterre and Flower Garden: June

I**N MID JUNE** inoculate Jasmine, Roses, and some other rare shrubs. Sow now also some Anemony-seeds. Take up your tulip-bulbs, burying such immediately as you find naked upon your beds; or else plant them in some cooler place; and refresh over-parch'd beds with water. Water your pots of Narcissus of Japan (that rare Flower) &c. Stop some of your Scabious from running to seed the first year, by now removing them and next year they will produce excellent flowers. Also may you now take up all such Plants and Flower-roots as endure not well out of the ground, and replant them again immediately; such as the early Cyclamen, Jacynth-Oriental, and other bulbous Jacynths, Iris, Fritillaria, Crown-Imperial, Martagon, Muscaris, Dens Canis &c.

KALENDARIUM HORTENSE: OR THE GARD'NER'S ALMANAC, JOHN EVELYN, 1659

Of Divers Other Flower-bearing Trees

T**HE DOUBLE BLOSSOMED POMEGRANATE TREE**, is esteemed the rarest of all Flowering Trees yielding so pleasant a Branch and a much more Lustrious Blossome.

This Tree deserves the choicest place in your Garden and under the warmest Wall, being tender whilst young, but after very hardy, the Flowers are double fair and beautiful, exceeding all others, born by Trees: they are easily propagated by Layers.

SYSTEMA HORTICULTURAE, OR THE ART OF GARDENING, JOHN WOOLRIDGE, 1677

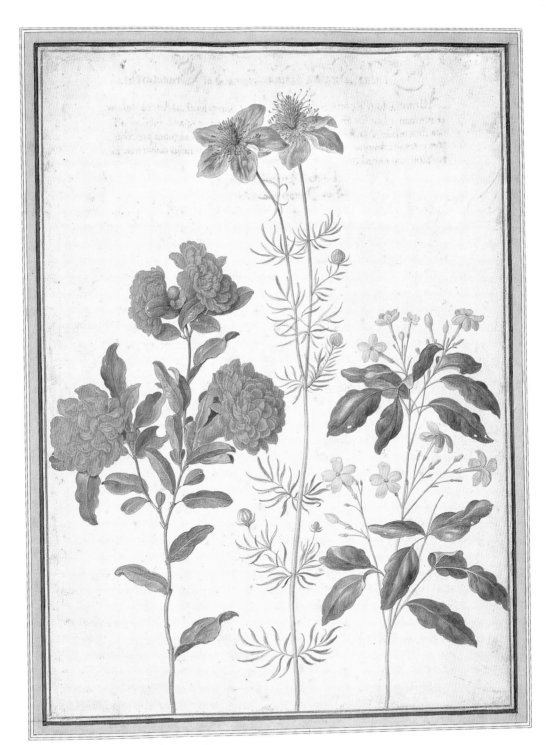

POMEGRANATE, A LOVE-IN-A-MIST, JASMINE

Lilies

OF LILLIES

THE MARTAGON IMPERIALL; The White Martagon; The White Spotted Martagon; The Blush Martagon; The Lesser Mountaine Lilly; The Spotted Martagon of Canada; all these Lillies have been found in the divers Countries of Germany, and are all made Denisons in our London Gardens, where they flourish as in their naturall places.

They flower about the latter end of June for the most part, yet the first springeth out of the ground a moneth at least before the other.

The Early Red Martagon; The Red Martagon of Constantinople; The Red Spotted Martagon of Constantinople; The Bright Red Martagon of Hungarie; The Yellow Spotted Martagon; The Gold and Red Lillies; The Dwarfe Red Lilly; The Gold Red Lilly; The Dwarfe bulbed Lilly; The Fierie Red bulbed Lilly; The Fierie Red double Lilly; The Greater bulbed Red Lilly.

These Lillies doe all grow in Gardens, but their naturall places of growing is the Mountaines and the Vallies neere them in Italy.

They flower for the most part in June.

PARADISI IN SOLE PARADISUS TERRESTRIS, JOHN PARKINSON, 1629

THE NYMPH COMPLAINING FOR THE DEATH OF HER FAUN

I HAVE A GARDEN OF MY OWN,
But so with Roses over grown,
And Lillies, that you would it guess
To be a little Wilderness.
And all the spring time of the year
It onely loved to be there.
Among the beds of Lillyes, I
Have sought it oft, where it should lye;
Yet could not, till it self would rise,
Find it, although before mine Eyes.
For, in the flaxen Lillies shade,
It like a bank of Lillies laid.

Upon the Roses it would feed,
Upon its Lips ev'n seem'd to bleed:
And then to me 'twould boldly trip,
And print those Roses on my Lip.
But all its chief delight was still
On Roses thus its self to fill:
And its pure virgin Limbs to fold
In whitest sheets of Lillies cold.
Had it liv'd long, it would have been
Lillies without, Roses within.

ANDREW MARVELL (1621-78)

THE LILY

THE WHITE MADONNA LILY is considered to be one of the oldest of domesticated flowers: it is certainly one of the loveliest. Proof of its existence is given at 3000 BC, and visual evidence survives in the form of paintings on Cretan vases and objects from the Minoan perod, between 1750 and 1600 BC. Eastern Mediterranean civilisations also depicted this purest of flowers.

It is thought it originated in the Balkans, which leads to the possibility that the flower is a survivor from before the Quaternary Ice Age, when most of the rest of Europe's plant life was destroyed.

References in the Bible to lilies do not always apply to the lily, which was a word loosely used for any handsome flower. Italian and Flemish religious paintings however do have representations of the lily, as a symbol of the purity of the Virgin Mary. The flower became her special emblem, dating from the story of the Assumption, when apparently the apostles, on the third day after her interment, visited her tomb and found it open and filled with roses and lilies. According to the venerable Bede, the white petals symbolised the purity of the Virgin's body and the golden anthers the beauty of her soul.

The Romans cultivated the flower, named as *Lilium candidum* by the poet Virgil. It was probably the Romans who brought the lily to Britain.

Variations of lilies were grown in cultivation, one of which, introduced from Turkey was known as *Sultan Zambach* or 'King Jasmine'. Among the several different lilies in the paintings Johann Walther made at Idstein is this same flower, proof that it was in Europe in the mid-17th century. Walther also painted brightly coloured Martagon lilies which were introduced within the 16th and 17th centuries.

In the time of Gerard and Parkinson, in the early 17th century, *Lilium chalcedonicum,* the Scarlet Turk's Cap Lily had recently been introduced into their gardens, as Parkinson wrote 'the red Martagon of Constantinople is become so common everywhere, and so well known to all lovers of these delights, that I shall seem to them to loose time, to bestow many lines upon it; yet because it is so faire a flower, and was at the first so highly esteemed, it deserveth his place and commendations, howsoever increasing the plenty hath not made it dainty'.

Since the days of those early gardening pioneers, many other beautiful lilies have come to Europe via explorers and plantsmen, notably from China. *Lilium regale,* one of the finest, was only relatively recently discovered in 1904, found on the borders of China and Tibet, where it was seen blooming in tens of thousands in a wild and inaccessible valley, an unforgettable sight.

SWEET WILLIAM, LILY, CLEMATIS

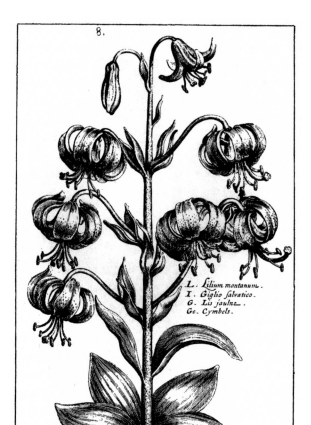

8.

L: *Lilium montanum*.
I. *Giglio salvatico*.
G. *Lis jaulne*.
Ge. *Cymbels*.

FROM HORTUS FLORIDUS, CRISPIN VAN DE PASSE, 1614

THE MOUNTAIN LILY

THIS WILD LILY called *Lilium montanum* puts forth rounded stems two cubits high or higher, long broad and pointed leaves not disposed one above another in uncertain order but at certain places on the stem, encompassing it in the form of a radiant star. The flowers hang downwards from their own stems, with the cleft of a lily, but smaller than in others, faded purple in colour and brilliant with purple speckles, the stamens in the centre being of the same colour. The petals are reflexed and turned backwards almost in a circle. The bulbous roots, like many kernels joined together, are of a golden or yellow colour (on account of which the French have called the whole plant by the name of *Lis jaune*), from which rootlets hang down. According to Fuchs and Gesner, it grows in woods and on mountains in many places in Germany. The Dutch have it with other lilies in their gardens. It flowers at about the beginning of June, preceding the white lilies.

HORTUS FLORIDUS, CRISPIN VAN DE PASSE, 1614

PERSIAN LILY

THIS PERSIAN OR SUSIAN LILY is certainly to be set down among exotic and foreign plants, nor is it very common but only found in the better cultivated gardens; it was kept by Dodonaeus among the False Hyacinths; it puts forth oblong greenish leaves less broad than the leaves of the other lilies, occupying the lower portion of the stem, and this straight round stem rises up to three, four or more feet in height, and its upper portion is clad and embellished with a large number of flowers hanging from stalks now longer now shorter. The flowers, consisting of five or six small petals, recall the shape of a little pendulous bell and represent most nearly the colour of dark violet, sometimes however approaching more to purple: they open not together but gradually and in a definite order, beginning, namely, below; they are quite lacking in scent. The root consists of a large bulb, in one part round, in another part flat, clinging to the ground by yellowish fibres at the basal portion.

HORTUS FLORIDUS, CRISPIN VAN DE PASSE, 1614

OF GARDENS OF PLEASURE

SO THAT WE MAY WITHOUT VANITY conclude that a Garden of pleasant Avenues, Walks, Fruits, Flowers, Grots, and other branches springing from it, well composed, is the only complete and permanent inanimate object of delight the world affords, ever complyng with our various and mutable Minds, feeding us and supplying our fancies with dayly Novels.

All curious pieces of Architecture, Limning, Painting or whatever else that seem pleasant to the eye or other senses at first sight or apprehension, at length become dull by too long acquaintance with them. But the pleasures of a Garden are every day renewed with the approaching *Aurora*.

While with succeeding Flow'rs the year is
  crown'd
Whose painted Leaves enamel all the ground,
Admire not them, but with more grateful
  Eyes
To Heaven look, and their great Maker prize.
In a calm night the Earth and Heaven agree.
There radiant Stars, here brighter Flow'rs we
  see.

Gardens, as if immortal ne'er decay,
And Fading Flow'rs to Fresher still give way.

(Rapinus)

*SYSTEMA HORTICULTURAE, OR THE ART OF GARDENING,
JOHN WOOLRIDGE, 1677*

Canna Indica flore rúbro.
Canna Indica lútea rúbris maculis púnctata.

TO CYNTHIA.
ON HER CHANGING.

DEAR *CYNTHIA*, THOUGH THOU BEAR'ST THE NAME
Of the pale Queen of night,
Who changing yet is still the same,
Renewing still her light:
Who monthly doth her selfe conceal,
And her bright face doth hide,
That she may to *Endymion* steal,
And kisse him unespide:

Do not thou so, not being sure,
When this thy beautie's gone,
Thou such another canst procure,
And wear it as thine owne,
For the by-sliding silent houres,
Conspiratours with grief,
May crop thy beauties lovely flowres,
Time being a slie thief:

Which with his wings will flie away,
And will returne no more;
As having got so rich a prey,
Nature can not restore;
Restore thou then, and do not waste
That beauty which is thine,
Cherish those glories which thou hast,
Let not grief make thee pine.

Think that the Lilly we behold
Or July-flower may
Flourish, although the mother mold
That bred them be away.
There is no cause, nor yet no sence,
That dainty fruits should rot,
Though the tree die, and wither, whence
The Apricots were got.

SIR FRANCIS KYNASTON (1587-1642)

CANNA INDICA

THIS PLANT WAS FIRST RECORDED by Clusius in his book
Rariorum . . . Stirpium per Hispanias Observatarum in 1576,
describing two hundred plants, new to him, found on a visit to Spain
and Portugal, where he first saw the Canna lily, brought over by the
Spanish from their West Indian territories. Clusius went on to
become one of Europe's foremost plantsmen, responsible for the first
introductions of many bulbs and seeds to Europe.

INDIAN SHOT

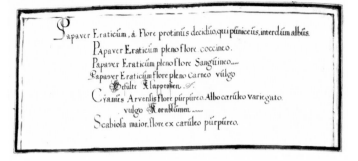

*Papaver Eraticum, flowers continuously, sometimes purpley red,
sometimes white.*

HORTI ITZTEINENSIS

OF FLOWERS
RAISED ONLY FROM
SEED

THE GREAT DIVERSITY OF FLOWERS we have hitherto had the pleasure to name may be propagated by divers other wayes according to their respective Natures, than by Seed, but there yet remain several Flowers not unworthy your care, that are raised by no other meanes than by Seed as the *Larkes-heels* or *Larkes-spurs*, whereof the *Tipt Rose Lark-spur* is the prime, is a very pretty Flower and well becomes your Walks in *July* and *August* or early if sown before Winter and defended from the most severe Frosts: they are generally sown in *April*, the best will degenerate being often sown in the same ground.

There is no Flower can be more glorious than the Poppy, were it as good as great, and as sweet as well coloured, and as lasting as it is nimble in growth, but their ill smell and soon fading, makes them the less regarded.

The *Musk Scabious* is one of the species of *Scabious* or *blew bottles*, and so named from its most pleasant scent, and called the *Sultan's Flower*, because the *Grand Seignior* affected to wear it in his *Turban*.

This though mean to the Eye, yet is a Plant worthy of place among your choicest Flowers, in kind years and good ground it will come up, being sown in *April* and flowers in *August*.

You may for the more certainty raise it in a hot bed, it is also said that if it be sown in *August*, the Plants will endure the Winter, and blow fair the next year.

SYSTEMA HORTICULTURAE, OR THE ART OF GARDENING,
JOHN WOOLRIDGE, 1677

CORNFLOWER, POPPY, SCABIOUS

OPIUM POPPY

PAPAVER

THE POPPY, the early 20th-century symbol of remembrance of the horror and appalling waste of the First World War, was for centuries known as a flower of sleep and oblivion. It was supposedly created by Somnus, the God of Sleep, to ease Ceres of her worries, for lack of sleep meant she was neglecting the corn. After she managed to sleep, the crops were revived. This is shown in depictions of Ceres, represented wearing garlands of corn mixed with poppies.

The Opium Poppy is the oldest species in cultivation: found wild all over the Mediterranean countries and the Middle East, its place of origin is unknown. It was known as a medicinal plant, not only as a narcotic, but also for its edible seeds. The athletes competing in the ancient Greek Olympic Games ate poppy seed mixed with wine and honey. Opium was made from the sap of the green seed-heads, known to have been in use several centuries before Christ. The pale mauve opium poppy was introduced to Britain by the Romans, and is a prolific self-seeder in gardens to this day, for purely decorative purposes.

At the start of the early 19th century opium was extensively grown in England: selling at 22 shillings a pound, it was estimated that 50,000 pounds annually were consumed. By the late 16th century garden varieties had begun to appear and by the middle of the 18th century many varieties were in circulation: 'Violet Poppy, Carnation Poppy, Curled Poppy, Fringed Poppy, Feathered Poppy etc, have been given to express their different varieties. Some are so finely variegated, their colours so opposite, and many so delightfully spotted that the finest carnation cannot excel them.' Thus not all poppies were for the purpose of producing opium.

Papaver orientale was found growing in Armenia by Tournefort, from where it was subsequently distributed to Holland and to England. Wild poppies, known as *Papaver rhoeas* were described in the 17th century as 'one of the most beautiful Flowers that can be imagin'd.'

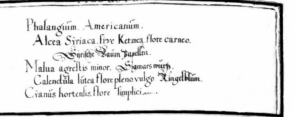

Phalangium Americanum.
Alcea Syriaca.sive Ketmea flore carneo.
Syrische Baum Papellen.
Malua agrestis minor. Siamurs wirtz.
Calendula lútea flore pleno vulgo Ringelblum.
Cyanus hortensis flore simplici.

MIDSUMMER FLOWERS

THE COMMON MALLOW was introduced to Britain by the Roman legions who occupied the country some two thousand years ago. The Romans used flowers for garlands and wreaths but also were aware of the medicinal and culinary properties of plants. They grew vegetables and herbs as well as the decorative plants that can be traced from representations in frescoes and mosaics left behind throughout their empire. Parkinson wrote mallows helped to 'make the body soluble; being outwardly applyed, they mollifie hard tumours and helpe to ease paines in divers parts of the body'.

Spiderwort, although known on the Continent before 1590, was named in Britain after John Tradescant as *Tradescantia virginiana*. Tradescant was an important figure in British garden history, introducing many trees, shrubs and flowers from his various plant-hunting expeditions to the New World, or buying trips to Europe. He worked for the first Earl of Salisbury at Hatfield House around 1609, before working for the Duke of Buckingham, King Charles I. Many new plants were sent to him from abroad, in particular as he was a shareholder of the Virginia Co., and was entitled to buy land there.

The marigold was supposedly so-called from a resemblance of its golden florets to rays of glory, thus was consecrated to the Virgin Mary, as Mary's gold. The name in Latin, *Calendula* means 'of the Kalends' because marigolds are to be found in bloom most months of the year. It is a useful herbal remedy to this day, and earlier medicinal uses are recorded from the 14th century, to cure 'pestilence' or 'feveres'. According to a 16th century herbal, garlands of 'mary gowles or ruddes' were made for feasts and weddings, and also it was used as a hair dye for those 'not beyinge content with the natural colour, which God hath gyven them'.

Dried petals were kept in Holland for use in broths and potions, and were popular as a cheap substitute for saffron. The single flower had the culinary properties, the double one the ornamental.

Parkinson grew the *Hibiscus syriacus* or 'Shrubble Mallow' as he called it not entirely successfully, as it was not sufficiently hardy, originating from warmer climes.

The *Centaurea* was named after Chiron the Centaur, as the flower supposedly healed the wounds from a poisoned arrow wound from Hercules. The wild cornflower has been another victim of modern farming methods and is becoming increasingly rare. *Centaurea moschata* or Sweet Sultan, came from Persia during the 17th century, where 'the Great Turke.....saw it abroade, liked it, and wore it himselfe'.

COMMON MALLOW, SPIDERWORT, POT MARIGOLD, SYRIAN KETMIA, A KNAPWEED

Carnations

IN THE PARTERRE AND FLOWER GARDEN: JULY

SLIP STOCKS, and other lignous Plants and Flowers: From henceforth to Michaelmas you may also lay Gillyflowers, and Carnations for Increase, leaving not above two, or three spindles for flowers, and nipping off superfluous buds, with supports, cradles, canes, or hoofes, to establish them against winds, and destroy Earwigs.

The Layers will (in a moneth or six weeks) strike root, being planted in a light loamy earth, mix'd with excellent rotten soil and sifted: plant six, or eight in a pot to save room in Winter: keep them well from too much Rains; yet water them in drouth, sparing the leaves: if it prove too wet, lay your pots side-long: but shade those which blow from the afternoon sun, as in the former Moneth.

KALENDARIUM HORTENSE : OR THE GARD'NER'S ALMANAC.
JOHN EVELYN, 1659

HOW TO PRESERVE FLOWERS BEING PLANTED FROM HURTFULL THINGS

THE WORST ENEMYES to gardens are Moles, Catts, Earwiggs, Snailes and Mice, and they must bee carefully destroyed, or all your labor all the year long is lost....

....Earewiggs hurt most Gilliflowers, and are taken best when they are newly podded (for they feed upon the young pods most) with sheepes hooves stucke upon stickes by the flowers, into which they creepe in the morning to hide themselves all day, feeding all night, and then you shall bee sure of them every morning and may easily kill them.

....Snayles does the leaste harme, and may bee taken in the night in the summer with a candle as they creepe about, or early in the morning, or after raine.

THE GARDEN BOOK OF SIR THOMAS HANMER, 1659

Caryophyllus commonly known as carnations.

A man who takes great pleasure in flowers
Will always be reminded of his own fragility.

HORTI ITZTEINENSIS

GREAT GILLIFLOWERS, OR CARNATIONS

THE STEMS OF THE LARGER *Caryophylleus flos* are smooth, rounded and jointed, a cubit high, or higher. The leaves are in pairs from each of the joints. They are oblong, hard, narrow, pointed at the ends, and almost of a bluish-grey in colour. The lovely flowers, in their long, rounded, and pronged cups, are usually of six petals in the single kinds, but in the double kinds of very many petals joined together, pliantly fringed and very much cut into. It is evident that those here portrayed show very great differences in the variety of their colours. The flowers have a very sweet scent, recalling the fragrant Indian cloves; and from the centre of the petals there project two clear white stigmas. The small, black seed is in little oblong vessels. The stringy roots endure for many years, and may be almost safe against the rigours of winter.

HORTUS FLORIDUS, CRISPIN VAN DE PASSE, 1614

CARNATIONS

MOUSE-EAR HAWKWEED, FOX-AND-CUBS, OLEANDER

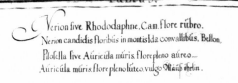

TENDER SHRUBS

Now, towards the end of april, you may Transplant, and Remove your tender Shrubs &c and spanish Jasmines, Myrtles, Oleanders, young Oranges, Cyclamen, Pomegranads, &c. But first let them begin to sprout; placing them a fort-night in the Shade; but about London it may be better to defer this work till mid-August: *vide* also May, from whence take Directions how to refresh and trim them.

Kalendarium Hortense : or the Gard'ner's Almanac, John Evelyn, 1659

THE ROSE BAY *

*(the old name for the pink-flowered Oleander)

Of the rose bay there are two sorts, one bearing crimson coloured flowers, which is more frequent, and the other white, which is more rare. They are so like in all other things, that they neede but one description for both. The stemme or trunke is many times with us as bigge at the bottome as a good mans thumbe, but growing up smaller, it divideth it selfe into branches, three for the most part comming from one joynt or place, and those branches againe doe likewise divide themselves into three other, and so by degrees from three to three, as long as it groweth: the lowest of these are bare of leaves, having shed or lost them by the cold of winters, keeping only leaves on the uppermost branches, which are long, and somewhat narrow, like in forme unto Peach leaves, but thicker, harder, and of a darke greene colour on the upperside, and yellowish greene underneath: at the tops of the young branches come forth the flowers, which in the one sort before they are open, are of an excellent crimson colour, and being blowen, consist of foure long and narrow leaves, round pointed, somewhat twining themselves, of a paler red colour, almost tending to a blush, and in the other are white, the greene leaves also being of a little fresher colour.

Paradisi in Sole Paradisus Terrestris,
John Parkinson, 1629

*Malva ab emolliendo ventre, nomen habet, etiam Plinio lib.20.
cap.21 monente: ideq propter naturalem lentorem suum, ut Paulus
asserit: unde à Martiali I.io Mollis vocatur. Latinis Malva &
Vasom quasi Molva, quod alvum molliat, qua antiqui in acetarius
cùm Lactuca ad alvum subducendam utebantur.
Malva hortensis, flore pleno, colore carneo. Pappel gefüllte Pendrosen.
Malva, rosea solio subrotundo, flore pleno.*

*T*HE HOLLYHOCK *takes its name from its soft centre, according to
Pliny, Book 20, Chapter 21 : and on account of its natural flexibility,
as Paulus asserts : Martial calls it soft (Book 1, Chapter 10) To the
Latins the hollyhock had healing properties, and was used for as an
emollient for curing stomach ailments. It was used with lettuce in
salads prepared with vinegar and oil (Pliny)*

HORTI ITZTEINENSIS

HOLLYHOCKES

T HE PLANT IS A KIND OF MALLOWES, and therefore
called in Latine *Malva Rosea*, the Mallow Rose. The
leaves are great and round, the stalke sometimes
three or four yards high, besett with faire flowers
from the middle to the tops.

Wee have single and dowble of these colors,
WHITE, PINKE, BLUSH, CARNATION, CRIMSON,
SCARLET, BLOOD RED, almost BLACKE, and pale
YELLOW, the Dowble of which last was rais'd by the
Duke of Orleans in France.

They flower in July and August.

The leaves dye down with the stalkes yearly, but
the rootes continue long in a good rich soyle, and a
warme place. The plant is fittest for courts or
spatious gardens, being soe great and stately.

Wee encrease them either from Rootes in the fall,
or Spring, or from their seed sowne in the Spring
which produces new sorts.

THE GARDEN BOOK OF SIR THOMAS HANMER, 1659

HOLLYHOCKS

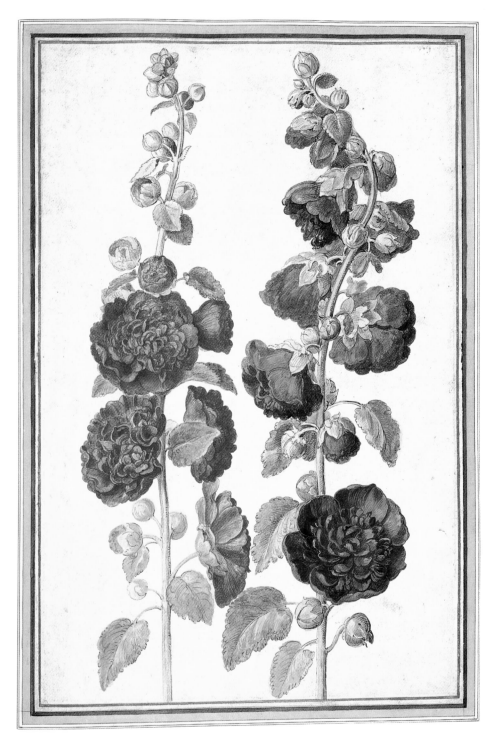

HOLLYHOCKS

Malva hortensis multiplici flore, colore incarnato.....
Malva hortensis flore pleno, colore atrorúbente:

OF FLOWERS RAISED ONLY FROM SEED

THE *HOLLYHOCKS* FAR EXCEED THE *POPPIES*, for their durableness and are very ornamental, especially the double, whereof there are various colours, they are sown one year and flower the next, they may be removed in *August* or *September*, from your seminary into their proper place of growth, which should be near some shelter from the Winds because of their height.

SYSTEMA HORTICULTURAE, OR THE ART OF GARDENING,
JOHN WOOLRIDGE, 1677

HOLLYHOCKS

THE ANGLO-SAXON WORD for a mallow was *Hoc*, and there is a suggestion that the 'holy-hoc' was first introduced around the time of the Crusades. Wild mallows grew in profusion in Palestine, so this is a possible link. It is hard to determine exactly what date it arrived, but the flower still grew wild in Persia in the 17th century, as recorded by Sir John Chardin, an Anglo-French traveller, who wrote admiringly of all the flowers he saw 'The flowers of Persia by the vivacity of their colours are generally handsomer than those in Europe and those of India. . . . There are beautiful marshmallows . . .'

These can most probably be interpreted as ancestors of today's hollyhock, and certainly Persian literature, miniature paintings and exquisite manuscript illustrations depict these, together with other favourite eastern plants: the iris, poppy, peony and rose.

Alcea rosea may possibly have come to Britain with the Huguenots, although Turner writes of 'our common holyoke' in his herbal published in 1551, long before their arrival.

Gerard wrote how single and double hollyhocks 'of many and sundry colours, yeeld out their flowers like Roses on their tall branches, like Trees, to sute you with flowers when almost you have no other, to grace out your garden.' Parkinson and Gerard both grew hollyhocks, as did Sir Thomas Hanmer, and by the late 18th century, Lord Burlington was raising hollyhocks in his London garden with seeds brought from China.

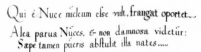

Qui è Nuce nucleum esse vult, frangat oportet...
Alea parua Nuces, & non damnosa videtur:
Sæpe tamen pueris abstulit illa nates....

THE SUNFLOWER
THE GOLDEN
FLOWER OF PERU,
OR THE FLOWER OF
THE SUNNE

THIS GOODLY AND STATELY PLANT, wherewith every one is now a dayes familiar, being of many sorts, both higher and lower, riseth up at the first like unto a Pompion with two leaves: at the toppe of the stalke standeth one great, large and broad flower, bowing downe the head unto the Sunne, and breaking forth from a great head, made of scaly greene leaves, like unto a great single Marigold.

There is no use in Physick with us, but that sometimes the heads of the Sunne Flower are dressed, and eaten as Hartichokes are, and are accounted of some to be good meate, but they are too strong for my taste.

PARADISI IN SOLE PARADISUS TERRESTRIS, JOHN PARKINSON, 1629

THE SUNFLOWER

KNOWN AND HELD IN HIGH ESTEEM as the emblem of the Sun God, the sunflower was originally a native of Western North America from whence it spread to Peru, where it was often found carved on Inca temples. It was described in the first book on the flora of the Americas in 1569. The seeds are rich both in protein and oil and to this day are used in cooking.

Syrian ketmia (a.k.a. rose of Sharon), sunflower

MARIGOLDS